LIFTING THE VEIL OF MENTAL ILLNESS

Published in cooperation with

CAMPHILL PUBLICATIONS, USA

224 Nantmeal Road
Glenmoore, PA 19343

Lifting the Veil of Mental Illness

An Approach to Anthroposophical Psychology

WILLIAM BENTO

SteinerBooks

Published in cooperation with Camphill Publications by
STEINERBOOKS
400 Main Street
Great Barrington, MA 01230
www.steinerbooks.org

Library of Congress Cataloging-in-Publication Data

Bento, William R.
  Lifting the veil of mental illness : an approach to anthroposophical psychology /
William R. Bento.
     p. cm.
  Includes bibliographical references.
  ISBN 0-88010-530-5
  1. Anthroposophical therapy. 2. Soul. 3. Anthroposophy. 4.
Astrosophy. 5. Mental illness. I. Title.
RZ409.7 .B468 2003
616.89'14—dc22

                                                              2003017027

CONTENTS

PREFACE

This book represents the core themes that developed over the course of five annual conferences held each February in Camphill communities from 1996 to 2000. These conferences were held to address the growing need of many therapists, nurses, psychologists, teachers, social therapists, and therapeutic educators to understand psychiatric and psychological issues from the perspective of an anthroposophical extension of medicine and psychology. Specifically, the Camphill communities in North America were encountering many more individuals with the dual diagnosis of mental illness and developmental disability, and they wished to collaborate with others to better understand how to work therapeutically with such individuals. This need spoke to the hearts of many individuals living outside Camphill.[1]

Over fifty people attended the first conference in 1996, and succeeding conferences drew seventy to eighty participants. The next four conferences each used the guiding images and physiological-spiritual archetypes of one of the four major organs—lung, liver, kidney, and heart—along with their associated soul disturbances. These five

---

1. The Camphill movement was founded in Scotland in 1940 by the Austrian doctor Karl König as a way to help children with learning disabilities within a residential setting. Camphill emphasizes community, both in a social and in a spiritual sense. Its methods and goals are based primarily on the ideas of Rudolf Steiner. Today there are Camphill communities for children and adults all over the world. See Michael Luxford, *Children with Special Needs: Rudolf Steiner's Ideas in Practice* and Rudolf Steiner, *Education for Special Needs: The Curative Education Course*.

conferences culminated in 2000 with a call to establish a seminar to deepen this work. As of 2002, the Psychosophy Seminar, with fifty participants, is in its second of four years.

This book and its companion, *Initiation or Aberration?*, do not attempt to provide a full rendering of these conferences but to publish the majority of lectures of the two main presenters: James A. Dyson, M.D., cofounder of the Park Atwood Clinic in England, and William Bento, anthroposophic lecturer and teacher. William Bento and James Dyson gave the keynote lectures that provided the basis for study and dialogue in each conference.

We are deeply grateful to the organizations that have made the publication of these lectures possible, particularly the Camphill Association of North America, the Carlo Pietzner Fund of the Camphill Foundation, and the Rudolf Steiner Foundation. We are also indebted to Dr. Michaela Glöckler and Dr. Paul Scharff for their steadfast accompaniment of this work and for their timely critiques and challenges.

In this centenary year of Karl König's birth, it is appropriate to recognize this book's debt to his pioneering work in developing the anthroposophic understanding of the twelve senses, the seven life processes, and the four major organs in relation to soul life and soul care. His work has been a continuing inspiration for lecturers and participants alike.

Gregg Davis and
Bernard Murphy
May 1, 2002

1. Psychotherapy in the Light of Anthroposophy

I have been on a journey, trying to develop what I call "psychosophy," based primarily on the leading indications Rudolf Steiner gave in Berlin in November 1910.[1] It was a time when Steiner was quite aware of the emerging need in the twentieth century to address soul phenomena. He attempted to bring a particular method of observation to these soul phenomena, a unique way of training that would allow one to bring the spiritual picture of the human being into practice. So he entitled this series of four talks "Psychosophy," meaning "the wisdom of the soul." He brought an anthroposophical, spiritual-scientific endeavor into the domain of psychology. Given the acceleration of psychology on its own, so little has been accomplished in this area that few stop to think about the larger basis on which we are addressing the phenomena of the soul. From an anthroposophical point of view, we try to take up a phenomenological observation of all the kingdoms of nature as well as the human being. These observations can allow us not only to perceive the human being in the kingdoms of nature but also to experience the human being as such.

Connected with these paths of observation is the path of cognition. We add to it an understanding of cosmology, the understanding that the human being, within the

---

1. Rudolf Steiner, *A Psychology of Body, Soul, and Spirit.*

kingdoms of nature, stands as a picture of the greater macrocosm. When these two ways of perceiving and experiencing the human being meet, the wisdom of the soul can be found. It is usually at a great price. We're not speaking about looking at something simply as a fixed picture. We need to look at these processes in life as a continuing dynamic, and thereby it requires a very dynamic and fluid way of thinking. Let us briefly contemplate a picture.

Let us begin with something that is very tangible that we have all experienced. We can experience the qualities of warmth in ourselves and in the world. We have the quality of warmth that is very much an inward sense. We use it even in the gestures of our language when we speak of feeling warmed. And then there is a very objective sense of warmth that is outside of this inner soul experience, the warmth that we meet in the world. If we look toward the source of this warmth and try to gain a sense of what it is that permeates the whole environment of warmth, we may turn our gaze to the Sun.

The Sun can be seen as a source of radiating warmth. If we keep our gaze toward the Sun, we can try to sense that, somehow coming from it, there is a whole sheath of warmth that surrounds us. We will also find light in the air, appearing as clouds. We also see color. If we are fortunate, some days we also see the whole spectrum of color, such as when gazing at the sky and seeing the changes in the atmosphere and clouds from morning till dusk. One might even see a rainbow. But what we're looking at is light. Light surrounds the whole sheath of the Earth. And even when the Sun is gone and the darkness descends, we can say darkness is intimately a part of light. We also can see the light of the night sky. Let me include here, just as a kind of metaphorical picture, a sense of the clouds as bearing a perception of light to us. These are visible and perceptible to us.

There are times when something descends toward us from the clouds: rain. We find the watery substance descending to the earth. And on the earth we find depositories of water everywhere: creeks, streams, rivers, lakes, oceans. But this is also a part of nature, and nature has a fluid, watery element. Let us picture the watery element, which can be seen descending as rain falling upon the earth, helping to create and enliven our earthly surrounding. Then we can gaze at the horizon, and we can see forms everywhere there. We see trees, landscape, mountains, valleys, and we have a greater sense of stability. All this is perceptible to us. We can paint a picture of it. Every day we can look out into the world and take a moment to see the vastness and the wholeness; we can see that these elements actually bear our life in such a way that they permeate us.

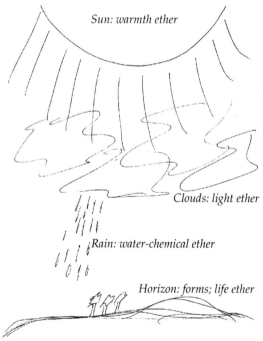

Sun: warmth ether

Clouds: light ether

Rain: water-chemical ether

Horizon: forms; life ether

Dr. James Dyson has spoken of the ethers: the warmth ether, the light ether, the chemical ether, and the ether of life.[2] These imaginations guide us to an understanding of how to place the human being into life. The human being cannot be seen abstracted or separated from this vast dimension of life processes that surround us.

We see the human being as substance as defined by form, and we know that it is the skeletal structure that provides this definition of the human form. The skeleton is the foundation upon which this human substance is able to fulfill itself and find its right shape. We perceive and feel this because it brings to our perception something quite definite and fixed as a form. We can think of the human form similar to the way we can think of the trees as a perception of nature.

But the human being is not merely a fixed form, standing statically before us with a definite contour. The human being has the capacity of movement, unlike the tree, which has its fixed form, or the plant, which stands there rooted to the earth. We would have to rise to the level of Imagination before we could truly perceive the human being that lives.[3] There is, within the human being, the whole watery nature. In this watery nature, so to speak, there is the fluid being, which is designated by the blood. The blood actually coagulates into what we call the muscles. But to merely say this is an abstraction; I have to really experience it. I can experience my movement, but I must bring to this experience an imaginative concept of

---

2. See James A. Dyson, *Initiation or Aberration? The Physiology and Diagnosis of Mental Illness*, based on lectures that accompanied those upon which this volume is based.

3. The words *Imagination, Inspiration,* and *Intuition* (capitalized) are used here as Rudolf Steiner used them—as sequential levels of spiritual development. See, for example, Rudolf Steiner, *A Psychology of Body, Soul, and Spirit*, "Pneumatosophy," lecture 3. These terms are capitalized here to distinguish them from their ordinary meaning.

how it comes about. there is more that occurs in this movement. I not only move physically with my muscles, but every inner aspect of me becomes a sense organ that moves out into the world—to take hold of the world, to take in light out of the world, to take in the air that surrounds me in the world.

So we know the human being is capable of taking in the outer world. And by taking this outer world into ourselves, all the processes of life that surround us stream into us and shape the inner life. It does not merely shape us as something static, but dynamic. This inner life is composed of the life processes, which stream in and shape our organs. If we were to bring this into cognition as a real experience, we'd have to listen deeply and hear how in this sensory activity there is a complete musicality to the inner life—music of the spheres, if you will. This experience requires Inspirational cognition. We are inspiriting the activities of the world into ourselves. Further, we can realize that the human being is not merely a receptacle for the outer world, but interacts with this world and has an inner activity. This inner activity is there within the streaming warmth carried by the blood to every aspect of the inner life. Out of this streaming comes the intention of our own self to become aware that we need the world; for we are the world.

We now have a picture of the human being that is not just a fixed and definite form connected to all other forms of nature as an earthly being. We see, physically, that the human being has a fluid nature, the etheric body. The human being also has an air body. That which is taken in as light in the air actually lives as the streaming interactive force that creates the possibilities for inner life and for soul life to take place. This is the astral body. Along with this warmth organism streaming in the blood is the ego organization, where we sense the act of will and the intention to become:

Fourfold Human Being:

warmth	blood	ego organization
air	breathing	astral organization
water	fluid	ether organization
earth	bone	physical organization

Form of body	skeleton
movement of body	muscles
inner lfe of body	organs
intention of body	blood

The picture I have built from the physical body started with a definite form of the bony system. Then I went to the muscular system, which I spoke of as congealed movement, and then I went to the capacity for the inner life. Organs are shaped in this inner life. Then we have the active inner life of the organs. We have seen that all the elements of the kingdoms of nature are to be found in a human being.

It is very obvious that with thought you can grasp the outer forms of phenomena. It's through perception itself that the basis of thought is given to us. But if we are to look deeper than the appearance that presents itself as a form, we would have to develop an inner life, an inner capacity for higher stages of cognition. I've intimated these as Imagination, Inspiration, and Intuition. It is by bringing our senses to pay attention and observe what surrounds us that we can realize that this fourfold picture is working into the human being. What I described as the ethers penetrate the fourfoldness that creates the human being for us.

If we can really penetrate and see the formation of both the physical and the etheric constitutions of the human being, we will see that they have a relationship to the internal organs. The internal organs maintain a particular form because they are deeply connected to the macrocosm, particularly to the planets. The lungs, for instance, are a more earthy component of our inner organs and are associated with the planetary rhythms and activities of Mercury. When we look to the planets, it is not merely to see them in space, because the planets in and of themselves have no activity. It is most significant to see the planets in their movement, and it requires time to see them not just in a position in the rhythms of time. It is the rhythms of Mercury that through time build up the organ we call the lung, which gives us the capacity to take hold of our perceptions, organize them, and bring them into some semblance of meaning. In other words, to bring about thought life. This happens because we are able to breathe in the world—its light, and all its fine ethereal substances.

If one looks at this rhythm, one of the vast mysteries of the macrocosm, we see that it takes Mercury eighty-eight days, or about three months, to go round the Sun. One can see that, if we were to follow the rhythm of Mercury throughout the whole year, we would see that Mercury has orbited the Sun four times. The Sun is the source of the warmth that streams in the human organism through the blood circulation. We know from our understanding of Waldorf pedagogy that education is all about teaching children how to truly breathe. In truly breathing, we develop a true capacity of thinking. This has to do with bringing the ratio of four to one into our physiology. For one breath there are four pulses of the blood. We have this cosmic picture presented to us in Mercury's relationship to the Sun, this ratio of four to one.

The liver is also an essential organ, a master organ that tastes the sweetness, the sourness, the bitterness, the saltiness of the streaming blood. The liver orchestrates the etheric life forces within the organism. The liver, in a macrocosmic way, is connected to the planetary rhythms of Jupiter, which takes approximately twelve years to

Lungs, liver, kidney, heart

orbit once around the Sun. During that twelve-year period, the liver matures. Only then, educationally, do we have the possibility of bringing about a different type of thinking in the child. One senses that the child now has the capacity to begin to discern life. This discernment is precisely what the liver is doing in sorting out the inner life. This discerning capacity of thought arises now in the maturation of the liver. The kidney is a very important organ, for it functions as the seat of the digestion of the life processes that we've been taking in through our senses. Just to organize perceptions is, in itself, not sufficient. It would merely be imitating what has been perceived. We have to take in our perceptions and digest them, make them our own.

The kidney functions as the seat of the astral body and for comprehension. It is connected with Venus. It's the seat of comprehension, because we take in the world and inwardly create meaning for ourselves. This creation of meaning is also mirrored in the cosmic rhythm of Venus, which takes nine months to go around the sun. We encounter the deeper mysteries of creation in the very fact that it is in this nine month period that we have taken up the embryonic journey, conceived out of love, in order to digest those things that we truly have love for. This is the mystery of the kidneys.

We will now complete this picture of building up the four inner organs, which reflect the fourfoldness of the human being. We now come to the heart, the realm created out of the circulation of the blood. It brings the whole cosmos out of the periphery into a center where our sense of self can awaken, giving us the ego organization. We know this rhythm is deeply connected with the Earth's year-long rotation around the Sun. We experience all the changes of the seasons; we experience all that is given to us as life processes on the Earth when we actively live into the year. This cycle is the marker of our biography. We speak about our biography in terms of years: when I was ten years, twenty years old, and so on. I'm trying to build a picture so that we can then go into the deeper questions of diagnosis.

I would like to take a leap. I have given you the physical fourfoldness and a bit of the etheric fourfoldness, and in the organs the fourfoldness of the astral body itself. It would be interesting now to contemplate the phenomena of nature. Let us contemplate the coming into being of ourselves, of what we call our humanness. We can imagine ourselves as spiritual individualities. From the very beginning of our journey, we are in the spiritual world. At a certain point, we experience a deep-seated intention to incarnate. This intention to incarnate is really a phenomenon of warmth. A tremendous warmth urges us to move out of the spiritual world, and this warmth is then illumined by the light. We can say this light is the firmament of the heavens. A sheath of light surrounds this warm intention for incarnation. Within this light live all the images in the zodiac, the archetypes of all the formative forces of existence. It surrounds us and brings to us our karma. And so, as warmth, we pass out of the spiritual world and through the starry world, gathering those imaginations that belong to what is essential and universally human. We gather that which is individually ourselves, including the pictures and the images of our karma that we placed into the spiritual world at the moment of our previous death. Our karma comes back to us and illuminates this starry world. Then we move through the planetary spheres, a continuation of a picture of our movement through the astral world. We then penetrate through the Moon sphere to find a human mother who bears the physical and etheric affinities upon which we can begin to work our way into this incarnation.

So you have a picture of the living spiritual individuality of warmth, later to be found in our heart as blood circulation. This moving warm blood takes its place in the uterus, where we find a home to begin the incarnating process. We go through all the planetary spheres. This act of warmth, or intention, develops courage in the spiritual world. We know it takes tremendous courage for souls to incarnate into this time, for we must bear not only our individual karma and destiny, but also the karma and destiny that face humanity at the beginning of this millennium. This courage leads us to enter life on the Earth. Once again you have this fourfoldness as a picture. One can take this as a kind of mantra in itself, one that brings us into incarnation. Then we spend our whole life attempting to remember this journey. We go through a kind of reverse current of remembering what was built up and intended in the planetary spheres as we came to Earth.

During the first seven years, the main forces that work into us are those that affect the growing physical body, but they also work intentionally to reenliven the whole nerve-sense system, including the brain. The whole task of the parent at that time is to protect and bring about a healthy exposure of the basic senses. After these etheric forces have streamed in for the growth of the child and have been released and freed up, then the years of education from seven to fourteen can begin. Here we come to the second primary portal. The first is the senses, the second, breathing, which is really the educational process. The third portal is then developed from fourteen to twenty-one, which provides a basis of being in the world. This third portal occurs between fourteen and twenty-one, when the astral body is finding its relationship to what has been built into the physical and etheric structure of the human being. It brings about a sentient awareness of oneself. The third portal has to do with physical digestion and the soul's comprehension that one has arrived on Earth.

This picture of incarnation, followed by life on Earth and then excarnation, is really a picture of the fundamental polarity of substance and spirit. You could say that the images are gathered up as fully as our time spent in the spiritual world was able to afford us. We gathered them and passed through the planetary spheres. What happens is that there are two streams that then descend. One stream bears the possibilities of perceiving the world through our nerve-sense system. All these karmic forces imprint themselves before our senses have completely synthesized. Our perception is remembering what we've met, but how we remember it is very much due to our own particular karma. So how we perceive the world is, if you will, predisposed in a certain way and lives in the nerve-sense system. It is the given substance; it goes directly into the hereditary body and the sheaths that our parents have provided for us. We bear this karma through, from race, to folk, to our parents.

Another stream arises out of the intention to move into the future. Let us call it destiny. Within our intention, we have a destination with a particular task in mind. That is what we love, and it calls us into incarnation. Love streams then into the blood. It is the given spirit. It is our past and a future that is given to us out of these two streams. What is not given to us is the present. We make the present, and out of the present, we have to make something of our lives.

These three portals have to be cultivated rightly before soul development can take place. We all know our being is attacked by the very nature of modernization, the whole technical orientation of today's civilization. But we have very little left of what we can truly call culture. Consequently, the basis of the soul life is attacked before the soul has acquired the faculties to take up its task in the world. Experiences that should not take place before twenty-one or so enter the souls of children who are impressionable and vulnerable to the world. The self-awareness that is working through the adolescent starts to find self-definition. In adolescence the whole struggle and striving is for an identity. This identity then is reborn out of a sense of our own ego, which starts to stream in at twenty-one. From twenty-one to twenty-eight, the possibility of an independent meeting with the world in a right way should take place. Up to this time, we have been meeting the world with our family, with our teachers, with our community. At twenty-one to twenty-eight, we begin to step out and meet the world for ourselves, on our own terms. This is the period during which the sentient soul development takes place, a soul awareness of forming our own relationship to the world.

From twenty-eight on, one tries to bring meaning to all of these encounters. We call the years from twenty-eight to thirty-five the time of mind soul. At this point, one can truly say, "I find truthfulness in how I meet the world, and I find truthfulness in how the world meets me." From thirty-five to forty-two, we have what is called consciousness soul, the sense of finding our will to bring about a transformation of the way we have found the world and the way we have found ourselves experiencing the world. If we have brought about this transformation both outside us and inside of us, then from forty-two to forty-nine, we can awaken to a period of time that connects us to our spirit self. Our soul can find its direct and right relationship with the spirit as it frees itself from the physicality of earthly being. [4]

In all these phases, we are meeting the actual workings of the spiritual hierarchies. From birth to age twenty-one,

---

4. Rudolf Steiner described seven components of the earthly human being: 1) physical body, 2) ether body, 3) sentient soul body, 4) mind soul, 5) spirit-filled consciousness soul, 6) life spirit, 7) spirit body. See *Theosophy*, pp. 56–61.

the third hierarchy of the Angels, Archangels, and Archai work to bring about these three portals that will allow the world in. From fourteen to thirty-five, the second hierarchy is at work, the hierarchy that wishes to bring wisdom and move wisdom into form; the Spirits of Wisdom, the Spirits of Movement, and the Spirits of Form. We begin to move with the soul life into the world, and if our education has been given to us properly, we will move into the forms of the world out of wisdom. In the last period, from twenty-eight to forty-nine, we encounter the deep working of the first hierarchy, the hierarchical beings that hold us to our word. Now the Spirits of Love, the Spirits of Harmony, the Spirits of Will are at work. This is where we must bring karmic fulfillment about in the incarnation; to really take hold of our intentions. They ask us, "Do you love to harmonize your will with your heavenly intention?" And only if we love to harmonize our will with our heavenly intention will anything of true significance come about.

In the professional work that I have been doing, I've been led by two streams that are only now beginning to become one. I found my way to Anthroposophy somewhat through the side door. It was out of genuine love and interest for astrology. This love and interest in astrology developed out of an excruciating antipathy and repulsion for psychology during my university years. I used to make a habit of taking my psychological textbooks and throwing them across the room. I thought there must be another picture or image of the human being that has some redeeming and spiritual, moral value. I found my way to astrology and all its various branches of cosmogony and metaphysics and occultism. It is only when I met Willi Sucher that I actually encountered something that spoke to my whole being. This search for a Christ-centered cosmology was livingly represented to me in this man. This led me to try to find what was the basis for astrosophy, and that opened the door to Anthroposophy. It is only through this that I had the courage to return to university to go through my education to become a psychotherapist. And now I am trying to unify astrosophy and that which is living as a stream of psychology, so they can live as one outlook, not as two separate things.

In the ancient mysteries, initiates went through a path of inner development. They had to train and educate themselves by learning about wisdom. One could say, in an imaginative sense, that the initiates, regardless of what culture or what time they were living in, deeply studied three books of wisdom. The first book was the Book of the Stars. The whole cosmological picture was perceived as continually active, continually speaking; the true nature of the human being is silently spoken in the writing of the heavens. This Book of the Stars has the deepest and most intimate sense of the images of the heavenly human being within it. It has thereby created what we see today as the inner attitude of the priest, who beholds the mystery of the spirit that descends out of the heavenly world and that which we can bring back to the heavenly world out of our own spiritual dedication.

The second book was read by the very same initiate, and that is the Book of Natura, in which one read of all the mysteries of life on earth. This book was the training of the true physician. You will note that in ancient times the priest was also the physician. Priest and physician formed one and the same sacramental profession. The priest in the deepest understanding of the spiritual working, the physician in the deepest understanding of the sacramental substances that provide a healthy basis for this working

There is a third book read by the same initiate in training. This Book of Wisdom is the book of the human being. It led to an understanding of what the origin, the nature, and the destination of human life is all about. One could say these were the true philosophers, the lovers of the wisdom of development.

These three books were read to train one single individual, who was priest, physician, and philosopher in one. These books, we could say, are *Astro-Sophia*, the Book of the Stars; *Gaia-Sophia*, the Book of Nature; and *Anthropo-Sophia*, the Book of the Human Being. These books have been separated, fragmented, and lost to our time. These three books of wisdom were last studied as one in the fifteenth century, when no physicians worth their salt would intervene or operate if they had not consulted the rhythms of the starry world. A physician taking up an activity of intervention was always there to understand the life of the human being, because they lived in the community with other human beings, understood their biography intimately, and were able to impart a philosophical word or two about health, mission, and destiny.

After the fifteenth century, we lose this. It's as if these three books are fragmented, torn asunder. For five hundred years we've lived with a continued fragmentation in all these endeavors, even in the realm of the physician. You may go and see a foot specialist, as opposed to an ear, eye, or nose specialist. Even in the realm of the priesthood, we now have the secular priest, the psychologist. You may see a psychologist for depression; another may be better for sleep disorders.

We compartmentalize branches of knowledge, and wisdom is hardly noticeable. The task of Anthroposophy is to bring a unified stream of wisdom and redeem what has fallen away in the Book of Natura. The Book of Natura, in its higher sense, is alchemy, the alchemy that was always present and known in various forms. I hope it will be the mission of astrosophy to redeem the Book of Stars, which has fallen into decadence as astrology. These are stages of development that will take many, many generations and centuries; but it is the task of Anthroposophy, out of the wisdom of the human being, to be able to redeem these books and bind them once again as one.

Psychosophy will be a practice akin to what is today being striven for as part of the new paradigm in psychology. To meet the extraordinary conditions that the human soul is facing today, many psychologists are returning to metaphysical, religious, and spiritual ideas in order to spiritualize psychology, which has been perceived as ineffectual and somewhat decadent. It, too, will be an approach that is fourfold.

The first approach requires that we train our attention for observation. Out of this, we will be able to see symptoms—those tendencies that begin to deviate from a healthy balance in life. Problems arise when symptoms become extreme. So we observe symptoms, and we try to put together a picture of why they are occurring.

The second stage is diagnosis. How do we come to diagnosis? There is no diagnosis without true attentiveness. This is a fundamental issue, but you will not believe how assumptions are made. Many psychiatrists think they know what they are diagnosing, because they have been taught to follow a manual that gives them criteria. Diagnosis means "a way through knowing." But this way through knowing is really about a worldview, and our worldview is absolutely essential when we try to know something. It is not only our own outlook that we need to know. Your client's whole biography is one of trying to know. Regardless of how problematic it may seem, we need to know and honor the client's way of knowing. So diagnosis involves two worldviews coming to meet, and in this meeting, one can begin to understand the causes of the symptom. The more we know the cause, and the more we understand the other through an ideal sense of humanness, the more we can imagine a prognosis for the cure.

That is the third stage. What is possible? How will it be implemented? The fourth stage, after prognosis, is the prescription, whether it's a strategy of counseling, an intervention, or a medicine. We can distinguish these four steps of activity in psychosophy from today's bio-chemical model in medicine and the biochemical model in psychology. The conventional way of going through these stages is a very simple cause and effect method. If there is an effect of an illness, there must be a cause. So we can understand the cause and effect of a new situation. It's a linear kind of logic. In psychosophy, it does not matter so much how well trained you are in exoteric matters, or even how much you know of Anthroposophy esoterically, of all these things connecting the kidney and Venus, and so on. All this must fall away. If you are to have a will to heal, the only thing that will really matter is your inner moral development. And here we need to introduce moral logic. Moral logic does not function on the basis of cause and effect. Cause and effect is the linear approach that says, "Something happened here, and now it occurs here." In our moral logic, we would use an understanding of time quite differently.

If we picture etheric memory streaming out of the past and the stream of the astral body, bearing intention, streaming out of the future, then we see that the principle of cause and effect is not linear but dynamic. The cause of a certain illness may have nothing to do with the past and everything to do with the future. Here we break free of this rather empirical cause and effect model. These four stages are not that new. In a certain way, they have been given to us from great teachers in the past. We know the four noble truths of the Buddha went through these stages. The Buddha looked into the world and he said, "I see the symptoms of humanity. The symptom of humanity is that all of humanity is suffering. Therefore, all human life is about suffering." His diagnosis was: this suffering has come to humanity because of selfish desires. His prognosis: if we were to extinguish selfish desires, then we would extinguish suffering. His prescription was the way of purification; that which we find in the noble eightfold path of the Buddha. This comes to us as a universal truth out of the East.

We also have this in the West, in a philosopher like Plato, who says: "The symptom is that humanity is really living out of vices." The diagnosis he made: humans live out their vices because they are ignorant, and they have forgotten the virtues that they brought with them out of the heavenly world. This ignorance is forgetfulness. And so people do not know how to distinguish between vice and virtue. His prognosis was to bring about virtue fully. Through educating virtue, Plato attempted to extinguish vice. The intervention to teach virtue, to teach the way of knowledge, was the basis of his philosophy—that is, love of wisdom. What is wisdom? What is courage? What is temperance? What is justice? These were not mere rhetorical questions, but actual remedies for the soul's forgetfulness. So in both East and West, this fourfold method has provided a basis of looking into the mysteries of human life on Earth. These mysteries present themselves when our soul experiences suffering, or when our soul experiences a sense of vice, or in its extreme, a sense of evil. Psychology has been built on these fourfold steps of coming to terms with the world and with the human being.

In terms of its history, psychology is actually in its infancy. You can say psychology is the child of philosophy. It comes about out of an utter necessity, because philosophy has grown old and has begun, in its own constitution, to degenerate and decay. Its last golden years could be seen in the fifteenth century, but if you march with history and look at philosophy from the 1960s to the 1980s, you find we are marching into the abyss. We have arrived, and from the abyss must come a growing love for what can emerge in this infant child of psychology. We must hope it will grasp the spiritual significance of human life once again.

I will now put it in a historical framework for you. If you see how the philosophers looked at human life and described it, they also were acting and perceiving out of these four stages. Take for instance Renè Descartes' view of life, particularly in his discourses on method, on a way of knowing. Descartes' interest was to introduce a new way of knowing. He says that it is symptomatic of human beings that you can never be sure of your perceptions. We have complete uncertainty of our perceptions. In fact, he said the epistemological basis of knowing is to doubt all your perceptions. The cause of this doubting, which we are now going through today, is that we have been using an ineffectual method of knowing; that is, we have used the knowing that has been given to us as faith from religious life. Now we are at the age of freedom in which we can put aside faith and religious foundations and begin to think on our own terms.

Francis Bacon takes this scientific methodology to heart, and says, "The symptom of humanity, the real problem, is that humanity has no capacity to predict nature." The unpredictability of nature struck Francis Bacon very strongly. He said this unpredictability of nature, both outwardly and inside ourselves, must be overcome. The diagnosis he makes is that we lack knowledge of nature and must gain it. Bacon says we must rip the Book of Natura from her and read her secrets. He actually states that human beings must put nature on the rack and torture her secrets from her. This, however, is the language of hate and envy. It says, nature has something I don't have and I must obtain it. If we can predict nature, then we'd have what we're looking for as a prognosis. And so the prescription is to torture nature until we have gained her laws, to manipulate nature until we can control it. Humanity has met the beast of hate through Francis Bacon. Descartes requires that we live through doubt of all our perceptions, of all creeds and dogmas. The prognosis is that certainty of thinking will come about by developing concepts, by developing theories that we can actually apply. As a new philosophy, he prescribes the scientific method of acquiring theories. So we have in Descartes a representative figure who says, "On your way to the abyss, first meet this being of doubt."

In his *Pensées,* the mathematician Blaise Pascal described another view taking place in this march.[5] He said, "The symptom that I see humanity suffering with is a sense of deep-seated fear. When I looked once into the heavens, I saw a spiritual world. I knew my God exists. Now I am told by modern science and philosophy that there are boundaries to knowledge, whereby I cannot know. This creates tremendous fear and angst in my soul." The diagnosis he makes is that we were all terrified by emptiness. We emptied the heavens of its spirituality by being in a certain solitude and silence. Pascal's prognosis was that we would need to instill hope in the future by breaking the boundaries of knowledge. And the only way to break boundaries of knowledge would be to one day anticipate that which lives in the religious life as a kind of spiritual knowing, uniting once again with what was developing as natural science. So here we have met the beast of fear along the way. By the nineteenth century, after four centuries of the march of philosophical development about human nature and the human soul, we are cast into the abyss, where we encounter these three beasts.

Sigmund Freud arises and has his own view. He basically says that the symptoms of human beings are described in the various neuroses, which, carried to their

---

5. Blaise Pascal (1623–1662), *Pensées* (Fayard/Armand Colin, 1992).

extreme, can become psychoses. The diagnosis he makes is that there is a kind of maladjustment to our life situations. This maladjustment has to do with forgetfulness. Freud states that we have been traumatized and have repressed things that unconsciously keep us in a perpetual state of anxiety. His prognosis is merely that human beings can adjust to the situation; they can cope. That is the best prognosis he can make, for what is done is done. His prescription, as we know, is a psychoanalytical technique of trying to delve into the unconscious and bring about memories. The error in this approach is that the only memories he is interested in are those that have to do with physical, sense-perceptible events on Earth. It is not the memory that Plato had hoped for. Plato envisioned that we would remember our virtues prior to birth, that we would align ourselves with these heavenly rhythms as a way of instilling virtue once again. This was not taken up by Freud. There is little trace of a Platonic appreciation in him, but a very materialistic way of thinking, a very lung-orientated way of thinking, and a kind of fixation of the neurosis.

Freud is not the only one who says we are in the abyss. Karl Marx does the same. His view of the symptom is that humanity as a collective suffers alienation and discontent. His diagnosis has to do with what he identifies as capitalism. He attributes it to a sense of isolation. The prognosis he makes is a classless society. The way in which we bring this about is through the communist revolution. Here, too, we see errors in this particular approach. It's a kind of misplaced understanding of isolation. Yes, there is indeed isolation in the economic world, but if we go further, where is the root of this isolation? It is the fact that human beings have isolated themselves from nature, but this is given little regard.

Perhaps Nietzsche speaks the loudest. At the end of the nineteenth century, he proclaims that humanity is living in the abyss and crossing the threshold. He looks and says, "The real difficulty and problem in humanity is that human beings are living in utter despair with a complete sense of boredom, and have really become purposeless." His diagnosis is that humanity is being lulled to sleep through the advance of civilization and its goal of happiness as a high virtue. It is humanity's own vanity that he diagnoses, the pride of believing that we can create a heaven on earth and live in comfort. His prognosis is that we should live a full and authentic life. We should find our way to becoming superhuman. And his prescription is that we would leap into a demigod dimension and create, out of superhumans, a superworld. We know how this ideology fell in a very dark way, in the 1930s and 1940s, in Nazism. Nietzsche's theory of the superhuman was not truly understood. The supersensible human being was not grasped totally, but only the outer garments of the supersensible human being that are expressed in the will and in the capacity to transform the world.

Rudolf Steiner stands at the beginning of the twentieth century and brings Anthroposophy. He says, "The symptom of humanity is that all of humankind is crossing the threshold of the spiritual world." This means the individual and the social world will be thrust into chaos. A tremendous separation of the sheaths and of the faculties of the soul will occur. Steiner's diagnosis is that this is the result of a materialistic worldview, which is inspiring an amoral technology built out of subnature, creating subhumanness in human beings. This subhuman quality expresses itself in mechanistic and animalistic forms. It is the signature of true evil in the world. Steiner's prognosis is to permeate humanity and bring about a spiritual worldview that, at its basis, places love and goodness at the center of the redemption of the times. His prescription is a path of meditatively acquired knowledge of the spiritual within the human being and the kingdoms of nature.

For those who are working in the field of counseling,
I would like to address the conventional bible of psychiatric diagnosis. It is called *The Diagnostic and Statistical Manual (DSM).*[6] It tells us how to observe the
human being's symptoms, and how many symptoms
there need to be as criteria for labeling a particular
pathology. It is based on five axes. These axes are all
given a particular definition. The first axis is where we
find major pathology, such as the indices of psychosis
or the major depressive affective disorders. The second
axis is called personality disorders. It's not personality
order, it's disorder. The third axis one hopes to find
(and one can only hope to find these days) is a sufficient medical history. On axis four are described the
psychosocial stressors, or possible causes of stress that
have resulted in a certain chaos and breakdown in the
soul (death of a wife, loss of job, and so on). Axis five is
called the global assessment of function. It addresses
the following questions: How well is this person func-
tioning? Can this person get up in the morning and
attend work? Is this person able to manage certain
basic necessities and independence? It is an axis that
sometimes needs no description. You can get a diagnosis that has only numbers. These numbers are coded to
give you the specificity of the pathology or personality
disorder, all based on an image of the human being
that is disordered or ill in the first place. So it is a training for observing only illness, with no counterbalance
of health. Second, it has this fixated way of looking
only at what it can quantify through number, measure,
and weight. It's a quantitative approach of observing
illness, and so the fullness of the true human being that
needs to be described is missing.

---

6. *Diagnostic and Statistical Manual of Mental Disorders: DSM-IV-TR.*

DSM IV:

Axis I 296.40	major psychopathology	spirit
Axis II 301.4	personality disorder	soul
Axis III none	medical history	body
Axis IV 4	psychosocial stressors	world/karma
Axis V 66	global assessment functioning	individual/destiny

In an anthroposophical approach, we might say that we would not want a psychotherapist to fixate in the pathology that is presented. But, in an anthroposophical paradigm, if there is a pathology, the first axis we should be looking at is the body, or physical constitution. Many pathologies have their seat in a particular organic dysfunction that disturbs the soul's ability to make sense of this world. If we start not with axis one but with axis three, certain interventions that use nutrition or medicines may very well ease the great stress that a soul is going through.

Axis two is about personality development, which involves the whole biographical context, to understand how the sheaths have been developed through a person's biography; how their soul forces have been able to work in their thinking, their feeling, their willing. You could say we're looking at a kind of breathing—the continual interaction in human development that gives the basis for our soul between the etheric and the astral body. They breathe apart every night and breathe back together every day. Is this person really integrated, in the sense of coping with the world, in the sense of manifesting intentions here? The axis of major pathology involves the occurrence of significant dysfunction. The ego organization and its intentions cannot find a right relationship to the sheaths, and as a consequence digestion and comprehension of life on Earth is markedly diminished.

One can see this in Rudolf Steiner's lectures contained in *Freud, Jung, and Spiritual Psychology*. What takes place

when one cannot fully incarnate? Why is it that fifty percent of Americans today cannot fully excarnate at night?
When fifty percent of the population turns to some form
of sedation to sleep, we know we have a cultural pathology. Even a very simple biological function cannot take
place in our time without aid. Just think of the ramifica-
tions of this. If sleep does not take place rightly for a long
enough time, you will eventually end up with enough
criteria to put you on axis one.

How do we review this particular approach? There is
no sense in throwing it away. It provides a framework for
observation, but there is no content or object for the
observation that is true. So we have to bring the imagination out of Anthroposophy into it. Axis four, the psychosocial stressors, is the environment in which soul
development can continue. In a Camphill community, or
in any other community, it would do no good for the psy-
chiatrist or a psychotherapist to work without involving
everybody who is in relationship to this person, thus trying to change the environment and lessen the stress.

I know that when someone comes into my office with a
problem, I am already contributing to axis four. What
will he think of me? Am I really that crazy? All of that
goes on with the patient. If you are truly involved in
meaningfully carrying another person's soul crises as a
therapist, then you know that the patient is not function-
ing at a level where the ego is present, because it is not
able to penetrate the sheaths. So the therapist steps in and
intervenes in karma and destiny, as an example and a
representative of an ego-being, who has interest, empathy, and love for the person's struggle. There is no way
around doing that. We must have interest born out of this
imagination: that every human being's mission is to
become sufficiently free from being bound into substance; to have a free relationship with substance, so that
individuals become free enough to love their incarnation.

2. OBSESSIONS, COMPULSIONS, AND ADDICTIONS: DISORDERS OF OUR TIME

At this point, I don't think we need additional concepts. But we do need to bring what we have into a kind of digestion, so that they can find a way to be expressed in our homes and workplaces. We have to practice these concepts because we have found them within ourselves. It is most important to find these things living within yourself. *And so, not dogmatic.*

I tried to present a view in the previous chapter that we can take in an anthroposophical orientation toward soul care in psychology. It is actually more akin to what is called sacramental counseling. In bringing Anthroposophy into the world as a movement of renewal for our culture, it was Rudolf Steiner's intention that every profession could be renewed. He brought something that would not negate but illumine and strengthen the capacity for all fields of work to reunite with the spirit. He even intended for spiritual science to bring certain professions to work together.

In a lecture cycle called *Broken Vessels*, we see his great hope that anthroposophical physicians would work in collaboration with priests.[1] And we can infer that he was speaking about those priests who had taken an interest in

---

1. An earlier edition was titled *Pastoral Medicine*. These were priests of the Christian Community, begun by anthroposophic Protestant and Catholic ministers to represent a renewal of Chrisitanity.

Anthroposophy—that is, the priests of the Christian Community. He also intended that, in this collaboration, the priest would not only be acquainted with the anthroposophical world outlook, but also have a deeper awareness of the cosmology that stands behind the process of incarnation—in the sense that the priest would be able to look at a human being's condition and situation and understand within these the working of karma and destiny. This is done primarily by understanding the relationship to the starry world: the planetary rhythms in their movement and their correspondences to human development. This is what destined Willi Sucher to work so hard to bring forward a new star wisdom. That star wisdom belongs in the realm of the priestly and the sacramental world. Its work needs to be supported by the physicians who attend to the bodily basis that allows us to have a soul and spiritual development.

So that is the idea behind an anthroposophical orientation to psychology. It is based on this witnessing of the potential divinity that the human being is destined to become and wants to bring to the Earth. Heaven on earth is a reality, because the spiritual hierarchies have already brought it here. We must unite with it again, but now in an entirely different way.

The laws and experiences of the spiritual world are to be found differently on the Earth, and when we find this, it is an awakening of wisdom. That which we love in the earth or in human development must be united with finding the laws of true development. We are concerned with the laws of human development and how we will have mental health through awareness and the wise practice of them. Without that, the dangers are increasing that mental illness will immediately confront us. But if we can meet this and bring this wisdom forward, then the whole task of incarnation is our offering. It is meant to be a part of the transubstantiation, which is something we do lovingly out of our own freedom. No one compels us to do it. It is something we must find freely as a kind of inner calling.

The New Jerusalem is a picture of this. It is already living there in the intentions of spiritual beings. There is an earth within heaven, and when we commune with the spiritual world, we witness what the spiritual hierarchies love. It is communion for them, a new force of nourishment. And so in the cycle that I have presented, we have this whole cycle of incarnation, death, and reincarnation. We are continually involved in this process. We are in the descent of incarnation, nurtured by the love of the hierarchies, which have given us the ethers and substances through which to have our development. From mid-life on, we must nurture the spiritual beings who await our participation in bringing our wisdom to light.

We also need to understand the workings of adversarial forces; these are the sinister deeds that are created out of an attempt to attack the sheaths we need for our development. Out of this "wisdom of knowing," the higher beings and the angels can provide us with the new faculties and capacities that will be needed at this stage of evolution.

I have already discussed the stages of development. I have talked about the brain from an embryological point of view and about seeing those gestures of embryological development as they relate to our ability to bring about a relationship to the world through our senses. How significant that is! A child or an infant is still living in the spiritual world. Small children have not entered the senses sufficiently to fully grasp hold of that which is in front of them as earthly reality. We know the infant has this realm in the back of the head, the fontanel region; it's actually rather soft. We know there is a wisdom in that region that must be protected. It is a region in which we could say the spiritual forces of warmth and interest stream, helping the human being remain connected with their pre-earthly intentions. The whole starry world is imprinted here. And it's important to realize that this is the realm in which the warmth of the spiritual world continues to stream and work and imprints into the brain the starry configuration from the moment of conception to birth. In this is contained the whole intention to meet karma and destiny. Not consciously but the imprint is there.

During the first three years of life, the spiritual hierarchies work out of warm interest and enthusiasm for human development. After that, we develop the sense that "I am here on Earth and I have established my sense of relationship to earthly space and enter into it for my own development in time." From that time forward, everything about human development has to do with the encounter of ego to ego. And even though a child's ego has not fully taken hold of the organism, it is important to recognize that a child's ego is a spiritual individuality as much as our own. It is not so healthy to meet an infant with too much sentimentality and baby talk. The child is beginning to discover how an ego being can speak, how an ego being can stand there in an upright gesture, and how an ego being is capable of taking hold of the world. The very early encounters that a child has with adults become a kind of transition from the loving nurturing still taking place through the spiritual beings to what can be transferred to adults. Is that loving nurturing taking place in the realm of the adult caregiver? As adult parents and caregivers, we step into a role that was previously taken up by the spiritual hierarchies.

We will see that this becomes increasingly significant in how we as adults will deal with those brothers and sisters who are struggling with obsessive-compulsive disorders (OCD) and how these lead to a withdrawal and cutting off their own ego, which is exaggerated in situations of addictions. We must continue to find a way to meet them as ego beings. But one may ask, What if there is no ego to meet? This is an important question and a tremendous challenge, and we can easily give up hope that addicts can actually find a way back to their core of spiritual individuality. We give up hope for someone who may be so disassociated that there are no real consistencies left to the sense of self.

Many of us probably have answered this question from time to time by saying, "I must give up, because I lack the capacity to meet it." At this point, this would be a legitimate, honest answer for most mental health practitioners, but it leads to the most important question of all: Do I give up on myself? Do I give up on developing faculties that I have not yet mastered? Everything about this pathology can be put in the context of developmental problems. Development is something we have come to embrace, and it never stops. Too often, we begin to relax and feel that we are what we are, and that is that. This attitude is a picture of our own shadow that leaps up in response to problems we cannot solve for others. They are what they are, and they will never change. What I am trying to convey is the idea that all these situations involve a development that I would call a parallel process—to the degree that, as therapists and healers, we are also involved in a path of development. We will, in some degree, be able to provide possibilities of development for these others, even if their development is so arrested that it is hardly discernable in this incarnation. However, we are not just working for an immediate resolution of problems for this incarnation. We are also working for the next incarnation, and I think those who work in Camphill communities know that very well. But that same attitude must go into the mainstream and break the shackles and the hindrances felt by those who are working in managed care, particularly those dealing with the deeper problems of addictions today.

How can a true ego-to-ego encounter take place? At one time, it was very clear that we had to find our center within ourselves, to refer all our experiences in life back to ourselves—to find a sense of ego. This was a rather new development 2,000 years ago, preceded by a mystery-school teaching aimed at finding one's inner core, or the "I." The task was to look into the world and see the phenomena of the created world—in plants, animals, weather—all as pictures of this developing sense of "I am in the world." Today, one might say, since the beginning of the twentieth century, that it is no longer a matter of being able to find the ego only at the center of one's own being. The ego will light up only in the encounter with other egos.

We can describe the threshold of sleep. We will leave aside the developmental thresholds of space, time, and consciousness. In sleep, there is a fear of meeting a judgment. Our ego development is intimately bound up with the ego development of others. These others, in the spiritual world, experienced a communion with us, because we have had relationships that bonded us soul-to-soul, and we have been responsible for knowing one another and illuminating the essential core of our being. Where mental illness or addiction strikes, we will see one phenomena that often happens. Individuals end up either in a self-imposed isolation or in one that is imposed in some degree by others. Think about this: the possibility for this new type of development for the ego is cut off when an individual is removed from a community that can provide the context to karmically meet those that may have something to offer and illuminate, or when a person is so deeply into an addiction that they isolate themselves from having any significant encounter with others. The ego is not really in the center, because it has not been illuminated. In the center is darkness. In the center is the void, the abyss, and we try to fill it up with various activities or substances. This is the surrogate sense of self that we try to find. This is the phenomena we are looking at in our culture.

The judgment we fear in sleep is not something that comes merely from other spiritual beings. They do respond to what we bring into the night, but the judgment ultimately lies with the Greater Guardian of the Threshold.[2] That is the being who has united himself with the ideal possibility of the divine human. We all have a certain access to this being and this being to us. This being does not need to speak at all, but is the light that illuminates us. In this illumination of what we have done during the day, we judge ourselves. The tendency is always to experience a judgment as being made by another toward us. This is very much the psychological issue in counseling. Somebody can easily say, "Well, I have been addicted to heroin because you just don't understand how my father treated me. There was no warm loving interest from him so my addiction is his fault." Once you have broken the hard shell of denial a little bit, you will find that the next stage is to blame others and not accept any accountability for the situation. Certainly, the father is a factor. But in this scenario there is still no ego to take responsibility for the choice of how to cope with the trauma.

The Greater Guardian gives us a particular opportunity every night by giving us the possibility of becoming more conscious in our soul and spiritual dimension. The whole task is to become conscious in the night so that we renew this primal experience that we had in the cosmic midnight.[3] I have put this whole sacramental journey in

---

2. See Rudolf Steiner, *How to Know Higher Worlds,* chapters 10 and 11.

3. "Cosmic midnight" is the mid-point of one's journey between earthly incarnations, the point at which one begins the return journey to a new life on Earth.

the largest context of life, birth, death, and reincarnation. But we know cycles are always capable of having sub-cycles, or microcosmic parallels. So this sacrament happens each day. Every day we can go to this midnight star and witness the Greater Guardian, but it would require the development of a particular consciousness. It would require the overcoming of the fear of the spiritual world. And that, probably more than anything else, Steiner had pointed to as the great hindrance in our culture—a fear of truly acknowledging and experiencing the spiritual world. It is a fear that arises even in those who know about the spiritual world. In fact, the more you know, the more reason you may have for encountering fear.

I see a lot of young people in Boulder, where I work in a high school; and they wear these statements on tee shirts and hats that say "NO FEAR." It has become a kind of mantra of the youth. It's a trademark (yes it is also a commodity that sells very well), but it is a message that is selling. The message is very rarely truly understood. It's put in a context that says "I'm strong, I can compete in this world." But overall, dismissing fear means that you have missed an opportunity for development. Think of times in your own lifes when you actually met fear. When it struck a physiological response in you, it went right down to the core of your being. It actually illuminated you for who you are in the moment. It can bring a certain honesty and self-examination of our development and capacities. Now, obviously, I am not encouraging that you go out and seek situations of fear. Although some are addicted to the risk of dangerous activities that give a kind of rush, they remain in this state and never cross the threshold. Wanting to be stimulated by fear is big with youth, and yet they come out of it with only a craving for more stimulation, and never get to the other side.

So the first threshold of sleep—and all the fears behind the sleep disorders so rampant today—really requires the courage to know and experience the spiritual world as having the possibility of encouraging inner development.

The second threshold is the soul phenomenon of awaking—to have the mood, the feeling, that somehow in the night there has been a judgment upon one's activities. The greater danger occurs as we come back from the spiritual world and have to cross the threshold from the other side. The last thing we will meet before we've penetrated back into our organism is what is called the Lesser Guardian of the Threshold, who has a tenacious memory for all the misdeeds that we have brought into the spiritual world. Here we have this experience of shame, this deep-rooted shame that the Lesser Guardian will say (and rightly so), "I am you." This identification is a faulty one, but if we have not schooled ourselves to understand the different laws of the spiritual world and the earthly world; if we have not schooled ourselves to discern true and false, then this false identification takes hold and sets a tone, a mood, for the entire day. The only way to really work through this encounter with the Lesser Guardian is to fortify oneself with what I will call a courageous discernment of truth. And the truth is that development is always possible, given you have an understanding and the will for it.

Then there is a third threshold that happens each day. This is the daily possibility of ego development—the encountering of another, particularly those that are new and unexpected. If we become so compulsively addicted to the fact that we want to orchestrate our day and be in complete control of it, then we will be not only sadly mistaken but quite deeply disturbed, because it doesn't work that way. That is not life and the reality we encounter. We no longer can just stay within our little village and meet the circle of forty or fifty people who are part of our life. People fly in from halfway around the world; new situations are emerging in every community every day, and

these situations are created by people only as a context to
meet you ego-to-ego. What will such meetings bring as a
new capacity? If we respond out of a compulsive angst,
and then act out this angst in some kind of rage, we miss
the opportunity for our own ego development. What is
this opportunity? What is this ego development about? It
is about embracing our karma and destiny. So many of
those who have fallen into addictions have resigned
themselves not to meet this opportunity. And then it
becomes difficult to really awaken an enthusiasm for
meeting destiny.

I would say that the only true foundation of intervention here is love. Not the sentiment of love, but the mystery of love. It will require that you sacrifice a great deal
of your time and energy merely to be present. It doesn't
mean you have a solution. But when we truly love, we
encounter the other. It is important that the other has a
sense that you have not given up on love. They are free to
participate in love with you or not. You are free then to
give what is possible. These are, no doubt, important virtues that were transmitted as the moral fiber of religious
life in our culture. But that religious life is falling away.
Even music was stripped out of its context, in a certain
way, so that much of what used to give us the innate possibility of moral development and moral forces is no
longer there. This has to be rediscovered. And this is the
importance of developing a path of initiation. Anthroposophy provides a path whereby we can develop faculties
that have yet to become common for humanity. We wish
to be part of the future.

Consider the physical constitution. Bodily development brings about three systems: the nerve-sense system,
the respiratory-circulatory system, and the metabolic-
lymph system. These provide the bodily basis for our
soul faculties of thinking (in the nerve-sense system), of
feeling (the respiratory-circulatory system), and willing

(with the metabolic-limb system). Yet we know that the human being is more than body and soul. It has been difficult for Western civilization in particular to really embrace the distinction between the soul and the spirit. In fact, we find this very clearly when we take up readings and studies that are in the mainstream of archetypal and spiritual psychology. The distinctions between soul and spirit are very thin, and at times, very misguided. Gender issues are even used to describe it—soul is feminine and spirit masculine. This is grasping for something. It's a striving. But it falls far short of a spiritual-scientific description of soul and spirit.

Human spirit is the activity of the essential individuality that came from spiritual worlds with intentions with resolves and wishes to bring about the transubstantiation of both body and soul. And so, even that which has been experienced and the soul holds and lives in, even those experiences are not finished. They must be transformed within us. Thus we have the possibility to develop our thinking in such a way that thinking is living. This kind of thinking is not tethered merely to factual information. It is not the kind of distorted thinking we've been connecting with the lung and the physical body or the life ether. Rather, we can really find our thinking in life—living thinking that moves. Like the chemical ether that lives in fluid, our thinking, as water, can nourish life. It gives life to others. There is something more to be experienced than "Where do I categorize this piece of information?"

This kind of thinking goes even further. If we've developed a living quality of thinking, we start to live in a world of ideas that we can see. A certain ability to see the world of ideas becomes possible for us from the realm out of which the ideas and the archetypes stream to us. We can actually go and see them, not merely in the night, but also in the day. This is the faculty of Imagination; a particular level of cognition whereby we live with the images that were the formative forces behind the created forms of our daily perception—that is, when our thinking is alive. If we start with saying, "I recognize it is a red chair," it really is dead. With feeling, if we can allow ourselves to stop that impulse of being judgmental or antipathetic, or even too sympathetic, and instead if our feeling life meets the world in all situations with a certain degree of openness, then we are connected with all that we meet in the world without judging it.

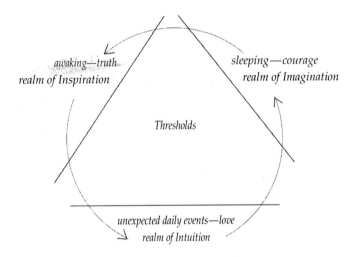

awaking—truth
realm of Inspiration

sleeping—courage
realm of Imagination

Thresholds

unexpected daily events—love
realm of Intuition

Thus we create a space in our feeling life for something to pour into us. This can be developed into the capacity of listening to all things. This is the cognitive capacity of Inspiration. You know that, as we hear music, we feel that it resonates into our whole inner being. It resonates particularly right into our muscular tone; moving muscles is all about inner music. If we begin to understand this resonance of tone in what is beyond merely the audible sound, we find there is a resonance we can call an after-tone. When we live in this after-tone, something entirely new can emerge. It is an Inspirational cognition I can experience that motivates me to bring this further into the world as creativity.

When our will activities are completely worked through and transformed, we are then able to have an intuitive cognition. If we really pay attention to what we do and how we experience things in life, and if we take the time to learn from this—seriously learn from it—after a while, something begins to emerge whereby we have an understanding of the consequences of our actions before we act. These are the seeds of an awakened conscience, and conscience lives out of this Intuitive knowing of what is going to result from any particular act. Intuition becomes, you could say, a prophetic type of consciousness, and it is a whole experience. We get in touch with our future activity in the world by being in touch with its consequences. We can actually think it, feel it, and touch it spiritually—this is Intuition. It happens in an instant.

We can train these faculties, and Rudolf Steiner has given many ways to do this.[4] However, we are in a culture that is distorting it by not allowing the luxury of time and space to develop this conscious faculty. It has to be done while in the world, in activities that are often thrust upon us, whether we like it or not. The subearthly forces indicate that there is a realm here of subearthly, bodily forces that are working right into the soul.[5]

---

4. See, for example, Rudolf Steiner *How to Know Higher Worlds*, chap. 2.
5. Uranus, Neptune, and Pluto represent cosmic forces involved in the formation of our solar system: cosmic light, cosmic sound, and cosmic life. Remnants of these formative forces remain trapped and condensed at the center of the Earth as electricity (light), magnetism (sound), and atomic power (life). These subearthly forces can affect human behavior negatively. (See Terry Boardman, "Uranus, Neptune and Pluto: The Three Magi at Humanity's Crossing of the Threshold" available at www.monju.pwp.blueyonder.co.uk/UNP.htm.)

When thinking is somehow impaired and is not able to reach out in perception to find a context of meaning in the environment or in situations, then there arises the wish to give up the attempt. An interest develops in something otherworldly. This is the addiction toward fantasy. The fantasy is, "I cannot really think my way through this world. I have not the courage to continually meet the fear of not understanding." This leads to a particular kind of addiction to hallucinogenics such as LSD, whereby the sheaths are loosened to such an extent that the ego swims in the world of cosmic ethers. The individual dissolves into a oneness in which everything is active, moving, and dynamic, but there is no center. There is no ego to it, and one becomes everything. The types of people who are more or less addicted to LSD and certain kinds of hallucinogenics find it very difficult to reconcile themselves to the century. And in their own being, an old memory gets distorted—an old memory that I would say belongs to previous incarnations we have all gone through.

There was a time when it was reasonable to have certain hallucinogenic substances as part of one's introduction to the spiritual world. These were parts of rituals and religious or spiritual paths of initiation. We have here a kind of distortion that becomes evil. What was good for evolution in one context and one period of time becomes evil when attempted in a time in which it does not belong. This is the evil by which the ego is being attacked and taken away from its development. It is a retrogressive experience.

A second type of addiction is sedation. When did a cultural interest in this type of addiction occur? Was it not in the 1960s? You can see there was the longing, through doing drugs, to cross the threshold of the spiritual world, because somehow the outer circumstances of life were not making sense or resonating with young people. A certain idealism was present—a pre-earthly idealism—that, after the tragedies of World War II, their task was to bring about peace, love, and a greater sense of brotherliness and sisterliness. These ideals were very hard for a teenager or a twenty-year-old to manifest, but they were very easy to experience together through drugs. It was a search for an Imagination of the spiritual world that was distorted by taking these particular drugs that created a premature loosening of the bodily sheaths.

Sedative drugs tend to be used when people experience difficulty in the realm of feeling, where the hypersensitivity of soul is so strong that any kind of disillusionment or any demands in interpersonal relationships, any wound, actually pushes them to withdraw from relationships altogether and to seek a feeling experience that is comforting—that is, as they remember it from infancy.

The drugs of sedation, we know have to do with opiates, but they also have to do with the warm, womb-like experiences of hashish or marijuana in this inner feeling of sensation. But this remains outside the context of developing relationships, of encountering the other ego. The hope was to find a new sense of feeling. To be inspired by these ideals, those in the 1960s sought a certain inspiration but lacked any capacity to act out of it. In the 1960s this realm of fantasy had a lot to do with drugs, so you could say this realm of sedation had a lot to do with music. The music is where they found their ideals reflected back to them. They felt that, if they could just surround themselves with the music, the world would change. But to take the messages of the music into the limbs was not so easily done. Looking at the metabolic-limb system (the will), where it is impeded or distorted and where one lacks the will to enter the world and bring about intentions, one seeks will substitutes. And these are the drugs that have to do with arousal.

One of the most important drugs that represents an addiction toward arousal in the will is cocaine. It has become a kind of power and status symbol, used rampantly and widely at high levels of corporate management by those who try to accomplish the almost impossible every day. It brings an ability to stay awake and a pseudo sense of power. To some it brings a certain feeling of being alive and being able to create change in the world. To make transubstantiation possible, one has to be alive with one's will, certainly. But this, too, has been distorted. In the 1960s it was distorted by the sensation of sex. And so you had drugs, rock and roll, and sex as the three addictions of that generation. Now we are experiencing the consequences of these distortions, which began as an attempt to develop spiritual imaginations, to receive spiritual inspirations, and to have an intuition of what life is all about.

We might ask how do these distortions happen? There are spiritual adversaries who are intent on creating hell on earth, who are willing to provide us with experiences of initiation, yet wish to eclipse any possible path of initiation. Soon, I think, this will create greater and greater tragedies in our civilization and culture. Yet there must be forerunners courageous enough to begin developing the faculties that belong to the future. We have to unite ourselves with the great forerunner who has the capacity to embody these highest of virtues—the virtues of true love, of wisdom, and of the capacity of free thought. This being is the Christ.

There is a figure that Steiner sculpted, the *Representative of Humanity*. There are two beings, one on each side. One is Lucifer, and the other Ahriman. Lucifer has the intention to obscure any possibility for us to unite with our higher being, our guardian angel. Lucifer wishes that evolution stop just where it is and be drawn back to earlier stages of development: the cosmic stages of development of ancient Saturn, the ancient Sun and the ancient Moon.[6] These stages of evolution gave us the development of our

sheaths, but not our ego, which is to be developed here on Earth.

So, yes, be physically endowed and have a sense of your life in your experiences, fill your ether body full of life, and live out your desires in your astral body. It is an interesting word, *desire*. Etymologically, it comes from the word *sidereal*, which refers to how we look at the stars. Sidereal time is true cosmic time, and the true sense of desire is, as Plato had said, those virtues that we experienced in our higher nature in the spiritual world. But we have forgotten them and have fallen into mere earthly desires. The greatest problem we have in our culture is to

---

6. For more on these stages of cosmic evolution, see Rudolf Steiner, *An Outline of Esoteric Science,* chapter 4.

sort out what we genuinely need in contrast to the desire and craving in us. A desire always wants more. It is a craving for more and more. Desires have a tendency to distort the imaginations and the wishes of the soul, because desires come strongly into our body as cravings out of subearthly inspirations. So, Lucifer, in a certain context, wishes to make us into automatons in whom there is no capacity of freedom to control our desires. Lucifer says, "If you have an instinct or impulse, just do it." That is the great cry of American culture: "Just do it!" Experience life to its fullest. And what happens is that Lucifer appears in place of the Greater Guardian as an image in your astral body. Lucifer attempts to create a pseudo-ego in the astral organism.

Ahriman works from the other side, so to speak. Ahriman has the greatest interest that we have no relationship to the natural worlds, but only to the nonorganic, synthetic substances of the subearthly. In this way, Ahriman will succeed when we have no capacity to enter the spiritual world and bring back something of it to the Earth. Then he creates his own kingdom. This kingdom that he has dominion over is a kingdom built out of subearthly forces, and we all live enchanted in it. Enchanted—we don't truly sleep into the spiritual world at night. We're sleeping in Ahriman's world. And so, you have these two adversarial beings, Lucifer and Ahriman, and working in the future, the Asuras will work to separate us from our true tasks, even from life. They will not just separate us from our higher nature, but eradicate our existence, whereby one will become nothing more than a crystal or mineral that will slowly, over the ages, dissolve and disappear from existence. This is the annihilation of human beings on the Earth. So we see the severity of these three adversarial beings working deeply in our time. Steiner had the greatest concern that we be prepared to meet this.

This is our larger imagination, but it is an important one for us to keep. What can we do as intervention? It is obvious that our starting point for learning how to intervene with compulsive disorders and addictions must be an accountability for our own inner development first. Are we willing to develop the new faculties that these problems demand? This has to do more with our own development, though some of what I have to say can be recommended for certain clients who may have the capacity to take it on. There are the levels that have to do with how one lives life on a day-to-day basis.

What we see with these problems is the person with obsessive-compulsive disorders is actually living in a fixed form of life in which the boundaries are so incredibly thick that there is no space for change or for other things. We all have a little bit of that in us. We have boundaries that we have to continually work on dissolving. It is important for us to find out how we restrict our movement, how we restrict our ability to allow things and space into our lives. One can look at this as something in the physical organism—how we create form in our life, how we write, whether we can from time to time tackle a new form of drawing that gets us out of our habitual way. There are little exercises we can do daily. We may ask, Where am I trapped in my own form? What can I do about it? Also there is this difficulty, particularly with addiction, in which one is constantly in states of denial and forgetting, forgetting again and again the source of one's trauma. It wears away the capacity to remember. It weakens the memory. The etheric body gets fixed, so that it is not able to move and take hold of things and retain them. So, we can exercise the memory by putting an object in a particular place every day, quite consciously, so that we can remember what we do each day. We will ourselves to be conscious. If we are not conscious of what we are doing, it is hard to have memory. A third exercise we could add is to recall the day. Not just to remember one thing in the day, but to remember the entire day in backward order. This develops the flexibility of one's thinking, but in this flexibility of thinking we have a kind of will to remember.

You could also look at how you have organized your space—your bedroom or your study. Are you willing to change something in it on a monthly basis? Are you going to accept change or does your room and your study remain the same forever? How can something new that you have experienced in life also be a part of that space? Changing habits is what we are talking about, so that things are not just done unconsciously and automatically in our lives. Maybe changing one's habit each month would be helpful.

Learning to distinguish our needs from our desires is also important. If you are not meeting your needs, and in some ways you have repressed them, they will surface again in a different way. If you are not meeting your needs, then you are involved in a type of repression. That can cause physiological problems in our organs, like the hardening of kidney stones or some other form eruption. We all experience this. You can take an inventory once a year or every six months of what you need for security and to feel empowered in your life, what you need out of relationships, and what you are doing with your lifestyle.

As you see, this whole situation of development is related to how we have orchestrated our lifestyle. It is based on our ideals and values. Obsessive-compulsive people have almost no option left in terms of their lifestyle. They do not create it; it creates them. Addicted people are created by the addiction. They lose control of their life. There are very simple things one can do—exercises to develop discernment for what is essential and what is non-essential. You can think, "I will not have judgments about my situation at work during the next month. I will try to hold back all my judgment and find out what it is that I am essentially interested in doing and what I am not." So we live with what is essential and we invest interest in it. Many of these individuals are bored and uninterested in the world, uninvested; they cannot distinguish what is essential from what is non-essential in their lives.

The more we do this inventory and this practice of inner development on a very practical level, the more we will be able to understand the other, and out of that the smallest little creative interventions can come about. And if we develop these higher faculties, then we may be able to see what is behind these problems. We can imagine what beast is unleashed to control their lives. We have a situation in which addiction and the attack on the ego is very much a matter of individuals who have been possessed by demonic beings. And we have to battle it. That is our task.

I would like to close with a verse by Karl König—and forgive me if I add a line to the verse, but it is within the context of this subject.

> There is a knighthood of the twentieth century, whose members do not ride through the darkness of physical forests as of old, but through forests of darkened minds. They are armed with a spiritual armor and an inner Sun makes them radiant. Out of them shines healing, healing that flows from the knowledge of the image of the human being as a spiritual being. They must create inner order, inner justice, peace and conviction in the darkness of our time. (They must learn to work side by side with angels.)

3. THE MYTHS OF DEPRESSION AND MANIA

What does Anthroposophy give us that we have enlivened sufficiently that it can shine out of us as something of light and healing? We know we don't have methodologies that we can simply take and use, and so we are left to depend upon one another to develop imaginations that create possibilities for a new approach to the deeper questions that humanity as a whole is dealing with today.

I have entitled this chapter "The Myths of Depression and Mania," but I really don't mean myth in the sense that I am giving it a secondary significance or slighting it as something other than real. The myths are realities, and the further back we go in time while trying to empathetically place ourselves in the consciousness of those who lived deeply out of the myths of their culture, the more we see that myths reveal a certain path of human development. And, with each path of human development there are significant dangers and hindrances that can eventually become what we call pathology.

I would like to start by entering into the Greek myths to give us a brief feeling of a different kind of consciousness, yet one that has concerns similar to ours about human development. All the Greek myths express a drama that has to do with the soul's search for the meaning of being human. In a certain way, the Greek myths have within them the seeds of what we will call goodness, beauty, and truth. These seeds later became the corner stones of what Greek culture gave to us at its height: philosophy.

Philosophia was the soul's longing to maintain a relationship with wisdom at a time when the evolution of humanity was such that the soul was descending deeper and deeper into matter—into the physical body and substance. There was already the prophetic warning from the spiritual beings in this that have been captured in myth, that humanity will now undergo a particular trial in which the guidance of spiritual beings would no longer be as directly accessible as it once was, and that in these trials, the human being would have to find new capacities. It is, after all, the whole meaning of evolution that we find new capacities of thought that allow us to find wisdom within a world of ideas that unites human beings. This is the basis of philosophy; a capacity to develop a healthy independence and emancipation, if you will, from the spiritual beings that once guided us. This shows itself in the great struggle to free ourselves from the theocracies of the past and to find what we know as individual freedom.

The required task for the Greek was to think and to bring thinking into a spiritual activity that would allow the human being to experience freedom. With this came tremendous challenges. These challenges, I would like to point out, have a great deal to do with the pathology implicitly contained in the myths. The Greek myths are, on the one hand, a story of the evolution of humanity, while, on the other, they are a clear prophetic warning of pathology. In the time of the ancient Greeks, if one suffered a tragedy that expressed itself as a physical or soul distress, one would have sought, as we would, someone with healing capacity. And often that healer could find a substance as medicament or find a way that one could take up a particular activity that would precipitate a healing process. But at times, the suffering and the pain was so deepseated that the healer knew this was still a task for the gods and goddesses. Through diagnoses, they would identify the symptoms of the suffering with the attributes of certain gods and goddesses and, as a result, send their patient on a pilgrimage to visit a divine sanctuary dedicated to a particular god or goddess.

The first requirement of the pilgrim was to bring an offering. This offering could have been the harvest of their crop or a service that they wished to perform for the mystery cult center they were appealing to. This offering, you might say, is a kind of placation of the god or goddess. Yet this is not the kind of interpretation I'd like to stand on. This offering is really the gesture in which the human being realizes, "I must reunite myself with the gods and goddesses so that divinity, spirituality, and sacredness return into my life." And so one makes an offering and is then given the possibility of knowledge that lived in a particular mystery center; which we would consider esoteric knowledge. If the offering was accepted, the person would be given a path of initiation. If that path was successfully taken up, the next task would then be to perform a service out of this knowledge, a task that, in itself, had the possibility of healing.

And so in the Greek culture there was a certain kind of therapy that involved esoteric knowledge, an awakening to a path of initiation, and certain rituals and sacraments that provided the possibility of healing. The Greeks had the word *therapeia*. Today, we think of therapy as very singly pointed to the concept of healing, but *therapeia* has a threefold meaning. It is not merely healing but also worship and service. The third meaning is healing. Worship and service preceded the healing. Of course, this involved a consciousness in which this "theotherapy" was quite understandable.

Fundamentally, the ancient Greek process of therapy was what we today would call the use of projection and interjection. The projection was "my pain, my suffering, my condition has something to do with my relationship to gods and goddesses, or spiritual beings. I must understand this so that I may realign my relationship to these spiritual beings.

Once one had entered something like an initiation process or mystery knowledge of this relationship to the gods and goddesses, the task for the priest or healer was to aid the seeker in developing an interjection of the highest attributes of this god or goddess; one absorbed the virtues of these spiritual beings. All of this required that the individual who was suffering would sacrifice self-interest for a time, in order to form a relationship with spiritual beings, albeit through certain priests or initiates.

I'd like to characterize this theotherapy more specifically in relationship to depression and mania. Using this healing process of the ancient Greeks as a kind of background, we can now delve into a couple of myths. Depression has an archetypal Greek myth, one that we know quite well. It is the myth of Demeter, Persephone, and Hades, or Pluto. It's a myth that is associated with a particular mystery cult of initiation in the Elysian Fields, an initiation that took place at a particular time of the year. It was a seasonal process of initiation that took place when the great fall harvest had been reaped and the time had come to withstand the dying away of life. Autumn would turn into the cold winter, when the journey into the underworld was enacted as a way to prepare the human soul for meeting the conditions that would ensue through the winter.

We know this myth concerns Demeter, the Earth Mother, who is concerned that human beings find a right relationship to the substances of the earth, in order to bring about agricultural harvests that bring nutrition, strength, and vitality to the human being. She had a young daughter, Persephone, and she tells her daughter that she can go and admire the flowers in the meadow, but that she should be attentive to everything around her and not wander too far. Nevertheless, Peresphone's tremendous love for what she finds in the beauty of nature distracts her from being attentive. She wanders far, and in one surprising moment, Pluto grasps her ankle and pulls her into his world of darkness—the Underworld. His treatment of her is not something we would call kind; she is coerced, exploited, raped, and made then to be his consort. This treatment creates tremendous despair, and in deep bereavement Demeter no longer gives to the farmers trying to tend the earth and survive. She bereaves, she grieves, and she falls into depression, because a part of her self has been lost. Peresphone has lost the innocence of her soul.

An appeal is made then to the gods and to Zeus. Something has to happen. Things are withering away and dying upon the earth because of Demeter's suffering. An agreement is made, and Peresphone is allowed for a time each year to surface and be with her mother upon the earth. But Peresphone has been transformed. The innocence of the soul has experienced the darkness of the earth. It has to develop new capacities—no longer the capacity of instinct, but now a capacity that is born of an experiential knowledge of the pain and suffering of incarnation.

This is a story that has depression within it. I'd like to mention another side, mania. This seems to be the other side of depression. We know that mania has the characteristic quality of an excessive drive in energy, a restless, compulsive activity. The Greeks had a particular picture of mania. There were many pictures of mania and many pictures of depression, but I am selecting only those I think are archetypal in terms of our understanding. I will speak of the myth of Pan. Pan is a goat-horned man who lives in the wilds and seems to live by the rhythms of the ever changing Moon. Pan has the deepest relationship to all of nature, in song, in festival, in dance, and in sensuality. Pan has no inhibitions. He exhibits a wanderlust and a tremendous need to have others engage in a frenzy of celebration.

The picture of mania was also present in other Greek myths, such as the myth of Adonis and of Artemesia. Such myths have more to do with what the human soul experiences as spring goes into summer, as life burgeons with sheer possibilities. So these myths were enacted at a time when instruction for the human soul was given to emancipate it from identification with the seasonal course of nature. This was done so that people would not die into depression during fall and winter and would not need to find release in the uninhibited abandonment of romanticism and spring enticements, but instead find a new quality of being human.

Our culture also has myths, and it has been suggested that the great myth of our time is narcissism. Humanity has reached a place where one could hardly imagine that narcissism could go any farther. In a certain way, the modern myth is the quest to master all the secrets and mysteries of the brain and the body in such a way that we can all be perfect. It says that, with all the modern innovations of science, medicine, and technology, we will one day eliminate suffering and illness. This is the popular myth of the superman. It is the myth that Nietzsche spoke so strongly about. It is a very narcissistic kind of identification. And on the other side, we have the myth that reality is only that which your sense perceptions can reveal to you: the reality of substance and form. Materialism has put a kind of spell on our consciousness, whereby materialism itself has become the only basis of reality. In this sense we find ourselves in a position to become godlike. Another part of this myth of narcissism says that we are the kings and queens of the earth. We assume it is our task to control and master it. So we become deeply attached to substances and forms, to sensory stimulation, and all that our sense perception gives us. In fact, we even become attached to one another. This has formed a culture of addiction. Western civilization is clearly a culture of addiction; it provides a mirror that we can turn on our ourselves as individuals. It is very difficult, however, to see what lies on the other side of the mirror.

There are also other myths that have to do with depression and mania. One common myth says that, if you are depressed, you are simply taking life too seriously. We hear others say "lighten up, take it easy." We know that this common platitude usually falls dead flat when we say it, yet there is a kind of ingrained attitude that this is the situation—that depressed people are taking life too seriously. Exposing this myth would show, in most cases, that precisely the opposite is true. Many depressed people are not taking life seriously enough, but taking life too lightly. They should get serious. In the case of mania, one has probably encountered serious realities without having been able to maintain equanimity. The frenzy, the anxiety, and the fear are coping mechanism.

Modern medicine also has myths about depression and mania. Aside from our popular cultural myths, we have this myth that all depression should really be understood as a biochemical phenomenon, leading to endogenous depression. And so the symptoms and the cure are sought through psychopharmacology. In the last eight years, seventeen million Americans have taken Prozac.[1] And we must add to this the many other kinds of prescriptions that others have taken for depression and mania. It is a fix-the-problem approach that modern

---

1. See, for example, Peter R. Breggin, *Talking Back to Prozac: What Doctors Aren't Telling You about Today's Most Controversial Drug.*

medicine and chemistry attempts. The other side of this myth, reactive depression, or depression that results from life's difficulties, suggests that we are all under tremendous psychosocial stresses. The implication is that, if we just learn to manage our time properly, we won't have so much stress; we won't be so burdened.

How do we build the deeper picture—one that is not swayed by the myths of our modern culture, but actually penetrates the realities? In the anthroposophical view, the human being is seen quite clearly in terms of a fourfold nature. I would like to speak of this fourfold nature of the human being in relationship to this issue of depression and mania.

First is the physical body. The physical body is not just a kind of extract or abstract of the spirit. The physical body *is* living spirit. This living spirit has life and activity. In the activity of the material body, our sense of living in physical reality has everything to do with the the liver, the organ of perception for life. The liver is an organ that perceives life and the processes of life, both within and outside ourselves. When it senses an irregularity or a dysfunction, we know that problems of depression and mania are quite likely to surface. Modern medicine points to chemistry and the brain. We know there is a link between chemistry and the brain, but where do we find the master chemist in the physical body? It is not the brain but the liver. We seek to open up avenues of more understanding and more research. What is this intimate chemical relationship that is in the fluids and in the blood of the human organism, giving too little or too much seratonin or some other chemical substance to the brain, and creating an altered sense of one's experience of life?

At the level of the etheric body, we are speaking of rhythms, particularly those rhythms connected to the liver's capacity to guide and orchestrate digestion. There are three realms of digestion: that which has to do with

substance; that which has to do with our sense perceptions; and that which has to do with the soul experiences
of sharing a common life, one to another, and how we'll
assimilate and digest what our life together is about.

In the astral body, the star body, the basis of our soul
life, images stream from the heavens into us. These also
affect depression and mania. It is in the soul that the
quest for meaning in one's biography takes place. Our
capacity to draw meaning out of our biography is based
fundamentally on our capacity of memory. Without
memory, we would be lost in terms of understanding our
biography. But if the soul forces of thinking, feeling, and
willing are separated, then you can be assured that memory will be disturbed, whether fixated and unable to
move from the past into the present, or fixated on fears of
things that have not happened. Time becomes disturbed,
and memory is really a kind of perception of time. We
often think of memory as that which is able to hold what
has been—namely the past—but we know that in the
astral body, time streams from the future. It has as much
to do with remembering our intentions as remembering
what we have done.

For the astral body and for the thinking life, it is very
important that in the field of counseling—where we
meet soul to soul—we can find ways to restore a person's faith that the world can still be a good place in
which to develop. It is also important to find ways to
bring about what I will call empathy and love for a person's biography. There is beauty in everyone's life, and
each pain and each suffering has a kind of gift that can be
unveiled if we form a relationship to that life. This can be
done only by awaking a feeling for these gifts instead of
avoiding the pain or turning away from a certain biographical situation. Then, of course, we must be encouragers of the will, encouragers of hope, that truth will
emerge if we dare to seek it. This is often referred to as

psychodynamic cognitive processing with another person and his or her biography. Soul-to-soul dialogue such as this is in the realm of the astral body. Deeper issues face us with the question of depression and mania, and in this we are concerned with the dislocation of the ego.

Where is the ego in a situation such as depression? All questions that have to do with the ego also have to do with the deeper spiritual issues of how karma and destiny are creating conditions for a person's evolution. And so we have to place ourselves rightly in relationship to a person's karma and destiny. This is one of the deepest and most sacred areas to address. Based on this fourfold imagination of the human being, we try to assess where depression or mania actually shows itself as a dysfunction or problem. Often it is at all levels, but at times it is important to know where the pain is. Where can I find an entry to be of help and assistance? Where can I bring therapy to the situation?

For those of us involved in Anthroposophy, our capacities have to be developed out of our own earnest path of inner development and through understanding the conditions of humanity's evolution today. So, I would like to say, we need to look at the conditions of the consciousness soul, which has been with us since the beginning of the fifteenth century. We need to look more deeply at this idea that "humanity is crossing the threshold of the spiritual world" and realize that this is incomplete unless we are also willing to say "humanity is crossing the threshold of subnature."

These phenomena must not remain for us merely as a set of ideas or abstractions. We must perceive this phenomenon. We must enter fully into the question of what it means for humanity to cross the threshold of the spiritual world. We will be clear then, out of our own experiences, that this crossing means that humanity has entered pathological conditions. The phenomenology of crossing the threshold of the spiritual world is simply pathology. And the more we can understand the pathology, the more we will see behind it the realities of the evolution of humanity and the demands upon every human being who is to pass through the conditions of modern consciousness. This brings us then to the path of initiation that is suitable for the consciousness soul. Every path of initiation must include aspects of the path I intimated for the Greek mystery cults.

Let us look now, in a fourfold way, at the conditions of the consciousness soul. The first condition of the consciousness soul involves the physical body, in particular, which becomes conscious through the apparatus of the brain. Consequently, the physical body is becoming more and more intelligent. This intelligence is united now with the deeper mysteries of the earth, inclusive of subnature. We think about creating an entirely new kingdom on the earth. We could call it the "kingdom of technopoly." This kingdom of technopoly goes further than what we've done with electricity and magnetism. Even now there are the first suggestions that we not only create outer forms of society, but that we also begin to create new entities within society. We can now clone life. These are very serious situations. We have gone so deeply into our physical body that it is very difficult to discern our humanness from the perspective of the materialistic view that says we are all part of the mechanistic mystery of the earth. In fact, we have young children doing nothing but imitating physical, mechanical apparatuses—not imitating the human being, but the creations that we have made.

This is the depth to which we have gone into materialism. We have gone into subnature, and the physical body is continually being stimulated by subnature, so that at times we are being stimulated unconsciously, moved by the stimulus of subnature. We take in the forces of electricity and magnatism. The nutrition we take in includes irradiated food, chemical additives, and so on. We are living with lifelessness. This is one characteristic. Will we be able to free ourselves from this identification with subnature? And yet, it's been an evolutionary necessity. We would not be able to have the wisdom of subnature unless we had the courage to commune with it. But do we have the courage to distinguish it from what we are to become?

The second phenomenon that creates a condition of the consciousness soul has to do with the fact that, as humanity crosses the threshold of the spiritual world, the etheric body loosens. The etheric sheath is very deeply connected to our sense of life and our ability to perceive life within our selves, and the loosening of this sheath is expanding. We then enter a realm in which we have a sense of living in two worlds. We begin to experience and sense the supersensible, and most of us do not have the concepts to understand this. But it is clear that more and more people are having these kinds of extraordinary supersensible experiences involving their environments and situations. This expansion of the etheric body means that we are being exposed to dimensions of experience that we really don't have a sufficient set of concepts and ideas to understand, so it remains in the realm of the unexplainable, the realm that disorients us and creates a certain confusion about life. Unless we develop concepts that allow us to meet this situation consciously, our sense of disorientation will increase. Unconsciously, this is the basis of mood disorders. It is the basis of perpetual feelings of anxiety, whereby we are never quite sure of what we are experiencing. Doubt then takes away the certainty of our own sense of being. We become split.

Third is the situation that has been taking place in the astral body in our time. The astral body is penetrating more deeply into the etheric and physical organism. This penetration of the astral body is a kind of burning light.

Images are bringing to us a sense that we now have to awaken to karma—not only to our own individual karma, but to the fact that we are inextricably bound up with one another's karma. What am I to do about your failings? How am I to take that as a responsibility? It can become overwhelming.

The divine images of human evolution live in the astral world, and they are becoming more and more accessible to our soul life. We can say these images stream from the Book of Revelations. The Apocalypse is being imprinted into the soul of every human being today, and we are powerless to do anything about this. It is a condition of the consciousness that we must pass through, and many of us suffer from this awareness.

A fourth condition concerns that which once gave us security in knowing who we were as human beings, which was given to us often by our culture and by the geographical location where we lived our life. It lived as an image of what a human being is. It was imprinted in our blood as an instinctive sense of humanity. This humanity has been dying, and in our time we might say this old instinctive sense of what it means to be human is dead. Something entirely new must be imprinted into our blood. A new sense of ego must develop, for the old no longer exists to give us a secure foundation for what it means to be human.

Jesaiah Ben-Aharon has spoken of this in terms of the heart, the central vortex of the blood, which carries within it images of the human being.[2] He said that these old images have dissolved, that the heart is empty, and that other forces now stream into this empty vacuum. This brings us to the question of evil. Whenever we consider pathology, we must also be able to discern from

---

2. See, for example, Jesaiah Ben-Aharon, *The New Experience of the Supersensible,* especially chapter 6.

whence this pathology comes. Behind it are deep moral, ethical questions of how evil exists within each individual. It is not merely something we project out there as someone else's problem. Rather, it is the deepest spiritual problem of the consciousness soul. How will we confront evil in our time? Our culture mirrors this constantly, day by day. This is a picture of the fourfold nature of the evolving human being, and because of those changes, many modern pathologies have emerged.

It would be good for us to take a moment to look at 1998, a long awaited year. Rudolf Steiner and others indicated many concerns about this year. The number 1998 is 3 times 666, which indicates a time during which anti-Christian forces—which must be related with evil—would be most active within human affairs. This is not simply a year during which such events take place; the process we find ourselves in has been going on during all of the twentieth century. However, 1998 could provide a moment of earnest reexamination and awaking to where this phenomenon is taking place within ourselves. How did it come about and how can we deal with it?

I'd like to give you two pictures that emphasize this before we turn to Anthroposophy as a path of modern initiation that can bring remedies to the situation.

We have to take this diagnosis to the core, if we can, and show that it really has to do with the entrance of evil into human affairs. At the beginning of the consciousness soul era in the fifteenth century, the task of humanity was to spiritualize the soul. The spiritualization of the soul required that we prepare for this crossing of the threshold of the spiritual world. In the beginning of this age, the etheric body had already begun to loosen from it's natural disposition in relationship to the physical body. This gradual loosening of the etheric body first took place in the realm of the head, and so a certain freedom of etheric forces became possible in the fifteenth century and for the following three hundred years, or approximately 1413 to 1713.

On the one hand the freeing up of these etheric forces allowed us to bring our thinking into the realm of Imagination, bringing with it possibilities that were not oriented to sense perceptions alone. Thinking could now develop a possibility of spiritual faculties, or supersensible perception. The gift of Imagination is one aspect of this. The other aspect is that it allowed the brain to go deeper into the earth in its intelligence and develop what we have today as the various forms of natural science. I am not placing a value judgment on either of these two developments, but they are phenomena of that time that we have inherited.

For the next three hundred years, from 1713 until 2013, a loosening of the etheric forces from the middle sphere of the human being has been taking place. This latter year is the most infamous, prophetic year of the Aztecs, the Mayans, Nostradamus, and others. Many prophets point to a turning point in human evolution in around 2013. Steiner's own reckoning is that, from 1713 to the end of the twentieth century, the etheric body will loosen itself from the rhythmic system, the realm of the heart, leaving a genuine sense of emptiness. This phenomenon also brings new capacities with it.

The loosening of the etheric forces as a sensory perception of life allows us to experience now the true interrelatedness that we all have with one another. My life has no meaning without yours. Living with one another is now the basis of our future. And so we have this new awareness about the social nature of life, for good or for bad. This awareness has awakened conscience, which is a faculty and the voice of the heart. It says, "We must become our brother's and sister's keeper for the welfare of our future, for our lives are now interdependent." The other side, of course, is that the heart can become empty and easily fill with other images of what it means to be human; our feeling life can become eclipsed or distorted, engendering a deep sense of despair and emptiness. So this loosening of the etheric body from the rhythmic system is the realm in which most of our pathology can be identified. In a certain way, the whole problem of depression and mania has been shown to be connected with an inability to breathe—an inability to breathe our soul in during the day and out again at night in sleep, and to commune with spiritual beings, which many of us have lost awareness of. Unconsciously, however, the human being cannot forget.

The fear of crossing the threshold of sleep is very widespread. It is one of the symptoms of depression. The symptom involves the inability to enter sleep peacefully or restfully because of various forms of insomnia. Consequently, during the day there are no vital forces to bring one's will into activity, because one has been exhausted by going against the current of sleep. Why? We know that in sleep we meet the spiritual beings who perceive us and what we have or have not done during the day. This judgment is a matter of fact, and so the depressed person spends a great deal of time trying to avoid the pain of this judgment and spends all day in self-judgment. The rhythm of sleeping and waking, which is again a part of this middle sphere, becomes unhealthy; and thus eating, breathing, and human relationships all become problematic.

This problem we experience with depression and mania because of the loosening etheric body also means that the liver needs the ego's activity. It can no longer do what it once did instinctively. The ego must be developed to deal with this phenomenon of the loosening etheric sheath, the fact of our expanded sense of self. In the astral body, on the other hand, the question has to do with the source of depression and mania. It begs us to be aware of our karma. Consciously or unconsciously, the question has come too close to each human being and cannot be avoided without our falling into serious pathological suffering and pain.

In the year 666, there was an arousing fervor toward the development of intelligence. In anthroposophical circles, we know this took place in the Middle East in an academy called Gondishapur.[3] It was a craving for intelligence that human beings could possess for their own use, without recognizing that our thinking life stands in relationship to the consciousness of spiritual beings, and that we owe a great deal of what we can think to spiritual beings. A certain evil of pride in intellectuality was already a seed in 666.

At the beginning of the fourteenth century, in 1332, or two time 666, the astral sheath was again penetrated by the forces of evil, this time in the realm of the middle sphere. This is related to the attack on the Knights Templar—the torture, the interrogation, and the suggestions to the Templars that their mission to bring the virtues of poverty, chastity, and obedience to social life were false. There were distorted suggestions of sexual behavior and of misuse of money and gold. The torture and suggestions forced them to escape the pain by excarnating from their astral body. Imprinted into them was the suggestion that, yes, you did do this. This form of evil separates the human soul from its biography.

Now we come to three times 666, in 1998, and the attack has to do with the will and how the astral body, in relationship to the will, can take up initiate volition. More and more we see the paralysis of will. In fact, our culture helps design this paralysis in the sense that we no longer need to use our limbs extensively. You can do all your

---

3. See Rudolf Steiner, *Three Streams in the Evolution of Mankind*, lecture of Oct. 10, 1918.

shopping from a computer. Your relationships can all take place on the Internet. All you need are your digital limbs!

We see that there is an image of the nonhuman that has been continually imprinted into human evolution. How are we to counter this culture of addiction, which has evil within it, working within each human individual? These conditions of the consciousness soul give rise to the pathologies of fear, shame, and despair.

The fear that we no longer have knowledge of life can be countered only by developing the knowledge of that life that we are experiencing across the threshold— knowledge of the spiritual world. We need an education of humanity that allows us to develop ideas and concepts to think *with* the etheric, not just about it—to know how to live harmoniously in the etheric realities of our life.

Second, Anthroposophy bears to us the possibility of understanding how to overcome shame—that is, the idea that the human being is in a process of evolution that requires reincarnation. This brings to us the possibility that we can work freely with karma and destiny. It is not a fact that will seal our evolution at the end of this life. But if we learn the laws of karma and destiny, we will no longer be overwhelmed by what it shows to us as the double that holds the memory of all our previous incarnations. Where does this double and the memory of former incarnations come from? In the astral body, it is imprinted into the head and the whole nerve-sense system. Everything that lives in sense perception is in a certain way a memory of previous incarnations. People see in the world something that catalyzes the memory of their failures from previous incarnations. So the conditions that we struggle with today in our civilization are conditions we helped create in a previous incarnation. What you see is what you have participated in creating. And this, if we see it fully enough, can be overwhelming. It is what we call the double that holds the previous incarnation's images before us. But most of this is below the threshold of consciousness. We have the sense perception, but not always the link in understanding that is associated with it. We will not be able, in this incarnation, to bring our ego into relationship with our destiny unless we see the need to awaken to what it is we are doing here.

The rhythmic sphere is being eclipsed and blocked out, because we are becoming isolated from one another by all forms of our culture. We do not really live with one another and share a common life. We all have our ever-so-private lives. We have bought into isolation. In isolation, it is very difficult to awaken to what your destiny is. It's not about your self-interest; your destiny is about the act of loving one another. We even have a culture that fears to be in a relationship.

Isolation of soul creates an underlying sense of depression, but we have a culture that mirrors this "glass plate" between us that we cannot seem to move through. We are thus stuck with the memories of all of our previous incarnations and their failures. We are fixated in the past and unable to find the present without one another. With each other, if we find the present, then we can take the responsibility to love, which is called transubstantiation. We can find common tasks with one another to transform the substances of earthly reality. This requires that we digest one another. We know how difficult that is, even in "karmic communities." Depression is really a conspiracy of the adversaries to isolate human beings from one another, so that we do not awaken to our pre-earthly intentions. We are then captured in the concept that we have to atone for all our incarnations by ourselves in this single life. This is an impossibility, but it is a clever plan of the adversaries. Not one of us will ever win that game.

We have to break this glass plate and find a way to bring the ego into the present. This requires someone who, with the ego, is in the present and interested in your suffering and pain. Only a human relationship can carry this true healing power. To overcome a culture of intellectuality and addiction, we need to create a counter culture in which human beings begin to exercise what humanness is.

A key to therapy in an anthroposophical approach to counseling, particularly when dealing with depression, has to do with understanding the person's biography. Biography is related to the life map that was scripted in pre-birth. We all have made intentions to meet certain situations of both karma and destiny. How we meet that is totally a matter of freedom, but we must understand and accept that these intentions are forces working in a person's biography. This means accepting responsibility for our own karma and destiny.

We need an education that is born out of a path of initiation, one that emphasizes pathology. Pathology is merely a symptom of the path of initiation. It is the path of initiation that we must hold up before each other. This path holds the ideal destination and aim. In listening to a person's biography, we have to bring to it a worship of the striving to become ideally human. There is an image of an ideal human, and we can say the forerunner of that ideal is the Christ. This worship means that, in every telling of a person's biography, every inquiry into a person's suffering and difficulty must become a sacramental consultation. In other words, whatever streams out of the mouth of someone in pain and suffering is sacred. In this attitude, we do not interpret or judge. We try to find a way to see in the pain and suffering and the striving to become an ideal human being—not the mistake, not the failure, but the striving to become fully human.

Second, as counselors and healers, we must have a sense of how to ask questions. Questions that awaken the will. This will has found a hindrance and become paralized. To awaken the will means we have to be able to formulate questions that stimulate an awakening, and these questions do not always need to be formulated by the counselor. Many questions will arise if we are able to guide our clients into particular artistic activities. For instance, why are these colors in your watercolor painting configured this way? Why are they this light?

Various activities can awaken questions of the self that direct questions cannot. We need to have the tact and the discernment to know how the will awakens. What are the questions and activities that will provoke questions for this client? So we create rituals. Eurythmy is a kind of ritual. If one is doing it therapeutically and rightly, there is a sacred element of the spirit and soul trying to find the right relationship with the body again.

Finally, I would say we need to awaken the sense of courage and cognition for the truth. It is this courage to strive for the truth that is the healing process. When a person discovers that truth, whether in your presence or somewhere else, healing takes place, because that person has found the being who is the Way, the Truth, and the Life of all of our being. He is the great physician, the great healer.

Steiner pointed out in *Broken Vessels*, a lecture cycle given to priests and physicians, that "healing will not ever be complete without the soul's ability to experience the sacrament of communion with others." In such a communion, the disarray of karma will be reordered. This karmic disarray is the pathology of our time. No healing will be complete without the sacrament of communion with others, which is the ordering of disarrayed karma, the deepest suffering of our time.

So how do we orchestrate the sacrament of communion one to another? We do not have Greek therapy, whereby we can find direct access to communion with the spiritual beings who, through the mysteries, guide us to our next step in evolution. Our path is through one another. Through striving together with others to form a relationship with the spiritual beings, we can receive confirmation of what it means to be ideally human. It is in this way that all therapies—cognitive, talking, artistic, and indeed all the auxiliary therapies that surround the physician's work—are meant to enter into sacramental life. In this way, we worship the suffering and the striving of every human being, because these are the symptoms of an effort to become more ideally human. We find ways to serve people by providing possibilities for them to awaken their will more fully and more vigorously, and by having the wisdom to know that healing is possible only when they enter with their will into life and take on a task. This is true whether one's task is vocational or having the courage to say "I will talk to my wife about the pain I feel she's causing me." Initiating the will is the beginning of healing. The completion of the healing is the communion that takes place because another human being was interested, cared, and loved the other person enough to evoke the possibilities of healing.

Our task is awakening the will to be here, now, not to be fixated on the past with this astral devil that says we are a failure. Our task is to encourage the feeling for development.

4. PSYCHOSIS OR INITIATION?

First, psychosis may arise as a result of attempts to cope with the pressure of too many sense perceptions, or undigested astrality.

Second, the signature of psychosis is that the soul's life becomes fragmented. Psychosis happens when the soul is not able to meet the world creatively. We all tend to be psychotic insofar as we do not take ownership of our incompleteness, our karma, our destiny.

Let us address the first characterization. Given that the kidney is related to the element of air, the light ether, and astrality, I would like to place before us the nature of the soul in this regard. To do this, we must first consider the nature of the sentient body. It is a body that has been impressed upon our physiology from the front to the back. Its forces "bore holes" into our head's frontal structure to create space for our sense organs. We see this in the eyes, which perform the function of sight, the nose, which performs the function of smell, and the mouth, which gives us the capacity for taste. These sense organs within the body have been imprinted to enable the soul to experience the world. Do we not have the common notion that the eyes are the windows of the soul?

The sentient soul, however, streams from the back to the front, forming the brain as a mirror to what the sentient body brings from the world of percepts. In the brain, we find the nerve-sense system, which gives to our entire sense organization the nature of intelligence—

the possibility of mental pictures. Alas, mental pictures are not in themselves intelligent. This possibility arises by virtue of the movement of the astral body, which may be characterized as the circulation of the blood.

I would like to identify this circulation of the blood in human beings as unique because of its basic movement of verticality (unlike that of animals). The working of the *gemüt* soul lives in this movement. It streams into the brain region and weaves the sentient body's percepts with the sentient soul's capacity for recognition. In this process, the *gemüt* soul endeavors to discern the true from the false, the essential from the nonessential. The consciousness soul streams in to permeate all three (sentient body, sentient soul, and gemüt soul) via the warmth of the blood. It is this ego force within the soul that acts to spiritualize all of these soul processes.

For the sake of completeness, we may add the gesture of the kidney-bladder-ureter-renal system, found in a similar form in the eye-ear-nose-throat system. This accounts for the ear as an organ that has an opening so that the soul can experience the world through sound. Recalling how the kidney embryologically originates in the throat region and then falls to the region of the sexual organs, we can sense how the fallen astral body is related to the kidney, but also how the organs of hearing via the ears may hold a key to the astral body that has not fallen.

Our entire system of sense organs can be considered a process of breathing sensory perceptions into our soul life. Imagine inhalation as the realm of perception, the held breath as the realm of concepts, and exhalation as the realm in which we expel the unessential and retain the essential to nourish our souls. Thus, exhalation can be considered the basis of memory. This soul breathing builds up the basis of our image building capacities—our thinking life. It does this through its intrinsic nature. The soul has three basic longings: to experience the world, to understand experiences, and to recreate the world on the basis of its intentions and, thereby, fulfill its destiny.

If this soul breathing is disturbed and does not take place in a rhythmic and harmonious way, then the signature of psychosis will set into the soul. This fragmentation of the soul life will appear in the soul's inbreath as hallucinations. These percepts arise not from the world of material objects, but from other realms. These realms may be organic or may be etheric or astral. During hallucinations, the objective context of meaning is not so evident, if it is present at all. The fragmentation that takes place during the soul's held breath appears as illusions, faulty concepts, and insubstantial identifications. In the soul's outbreath, the fragmentation takes on the character of fixation—ideas that lack movement. Often these take the form of cramps and fears, as in paranoid ideation.

The onset of these types of psychotic illusions are often found in the period between fourteen to twenty-eight years of age. Although a predisposition toward psychosis may be evident earlier in life, it is usually not diagnosed until this time. Interestingly, this time period is associated with the planetary influences of Venus, which is also linked to the organ of the kidney.

During the adolescent years, the sentient body comes to maturity, and a longing flames up in the soul to experience the world and all it has to offer. This flame in the soul is connected to ideals that have awakened from before birth. They are not usually conscious or articulated fully, but they are rarely experienced as intensely as they are during adolescence. It is the common bond of ideals that ties the young with a fervor rarely found again. To find it, one has to live one's ideals and find others willing to do the same. This is not necessarily a given situation in our time; we must creat it out of our own striving.

During the phase of twenty-one to twenty-eight years of age, the sentient soul comes to birth, bearing a sense of the incarnating ego. These years are influenced by the Sun and Venus. The Sun illuminates the venusian nature of the soul, shedding light on the soul's experiences in the world. The inability to assimilate these experiences is often a central factor in the precipitation of psychosis.

There is yet a third biographical phase of life during which Venus is influential—from forty-two to forty-nine years of age. Venus conjoins Mars to manifest one's ideal. It is the time when the astral body is transformed into *manas*, or "spirit self." It is also the time of the midlife crisis, wherein a tendency to regress to adolescent or sentient soul stages often takes place. Here, we might say a subtle form of psychosis can begin to invasively debilitate the soul from finding its true sense of destiny. As Dr. James Dyson has put it in one of his lectures, "Insofar as we do not take ownership of our incompleteness, our karma, our destiny, we all tend to be psychotic."

Working into the biographical phases of life are the pre-earthly experiences of the excarnating and incarnating soul. In the excarnating journey, we find that the third region of the soul is the planetary sphere of Venus. There, we bear in our astral body all the striving (or lack thereof) of our moral, religious life. All the efforts we have or have not made to develop a consciousness beyond the sense perceptible world is taken up by the Archai, or the Spirits of Personality. When our soul returns through this region on its descent toward incarnation, the karma of our moral, religious life will be imprinted into our astral body as unconscious instincts and drives. It is through these unconscious instincts and drives that we are led to encounter our karma upon the Earth.[1]

As we descend through the Venus sphere our souls are united with other souls who have an affinity with our

---

1. For a more detailed description of the soul's journey between death and rebirth, see Rudolf Steiner, *At Home in the Universe*.

own striving. We are thus brought into relationship with our karmic stream. Through the power of love, we unite and form an intimacy. This love is not of a personal, sentimental nature, but a high platonic love for a common striving and for the evolution of consciousness. In this planetary sphere of Venus, we vow to find one another upon the Earth and to awaken each other to our essential ideals in life. This is, in a certain sense, the supersensible fact behind the words of Martin Luther King, Jr.: "I cannot be what I ought to be unless you are what you can fully be, and you will not be what you ought to be until I have become fully what I can be." This soul intimacy of spiritual kinship is woven through and through with the power of love. It lives in our astral body as a longing to fulfill our pre-earthly ideals. It is both the desire and the wish—an inner striving to awaken our true motives for incarnation. Yet, the mystery of this venusian magic in our soul is that it requires human relationships to fully awaken and unfold its working.

Now what can we say of the workings of these Venus beings—the Archai? Let us look at Venus from an astronomical point of view. It has an orbit around the Sun in the form of an ellipse, in which its distance from the Sun changes. The orbital path of Venus defines the boundaries wherein the Archai work. At Venus' closest point to the Sun (Perihelion), the Archai create the karmic conditions upon the Earth for the development of the human soul. The perihelion point moves ever so slowly through the zodiac. This point was in the constellation of the Crab at the outset of the Post-Atlantean age and has remained within this constellation up to the present time.[2] What does this signify? The worldview of materialism—the

---

2. Steiner describes seven evolutionary epochs on Earth: Polarian; Hyperborean; Lemurian; Atlantean; Post-Atlantean (our present epoch); and two more to follow. See Rudolf Steiner, *Cosmic Memory*.

view that only form and substance have reality—streams in the constellation of the Crab.[3] The ancient Indian culture rejected this view, calling form and substance maya, an illusion. Yet the karmic conditions for the soul were nevertheless a reality; the soul was to descend fully into the body during the Post-Atlantean age. Thousands of years later, the Buddha was able to identify this condition of the soul and its fallen astral body. He identified all suffering as having its origin in desire and attachment to the temporal world of forms and substances.

During the time of the discovery of the planet Neptune in 1846, an extraordinary alignment of the orbital elements of Neptune and Venus occurred in the Crab (ascending node of Neptune and perihelion of Venus).[4] In the heavens a mighty spiritual event was taking place, a recapitulation of the war in heaven described by the events of the Old Moon.[5] There we find the origin of the fallen astral body, attributed to the influence of Lucifer. In the mid-nineteenth century, we find a second Fall. The Archangel Michael slays the Dragon and casts it upon the Earth. The Dragon is really a composition of animal forms expelled by humankind during the human evolutionary descent leading to the upright human form. This Dragon becomes the persona of Ahriman, who conducts a subsensible school inspiring the birth of a materialistic worldview—a

---

3. See Rudolf Steiner, *Human and Cosmic Thought.*

4. A node is an intersection point wherein two orbital spheres coincide. The ascending path of the orbit of a planet as it crosses the orbital path of another planet is called the ascending node. Perihelion is a term describing the point of an orbital path where a planet is closest to the Sun.

5. Using theosophical terms, Steiner referred to the immense periods of cosmic evolution as planetary spheres, not to be confused with the physical planets we see today. These are Saturn, Sun, Moon, Earth, Jupiter, Venus, and Vulcan. See Rudolf Steiner, *An Outline of Esoteric Science,* chapter 2.

la Marxism, Communism, and Darwinian theory. It is this worldview that has given power to the Dragon, which now breathes a world of technology into our midst.

In the heavens, the Archangel Michael conducts his school in a cultus that is a review of all the cosmic intelligence that guided mystery schools upon the Earth. During the mid-nineteenth century, students of Michael prepared to serve his reign as Spirit of the Time. Michael became Archai on November 11, 1879 as another extraordinary heavenly sign took place; the orbital elements of Venus and Mercury coincided (ascending node at Venus and perihelion of Mercury). The inclination of the orbits are called nodes. The Venus node in the constellation of the Bull, which it entered in 747 B.C. (the dawning of Philosophia), can be seen as the place where the Archai inspire new soul capacities for conscious evolution. In this case we are speaking about the worldview connected to the Bull—rationalism. Not as dry intellectuality, but as a thinking that can become the ability to see into the spirit world as well as the physical world; a true spiritual application of the Hermetic axiom "as above, so below."

These sketchy indications of the cosmological background of Venus can give us a sense for the time we live in and why there is such a battle for the soul. It becomes more apparent how Angels and demons live within each soul. For indeed all of humanity is crossing the threshold of the spiritual world. We are confronted with the choice between global psychosis or global initiation.

As souls who met in the Michael Cultus, we bear a responsibility to this world karma, and we must face the Dragon of technopoly. Only a meditative path aimed at strengthening the ego will give us the power to endure the fragmentation of the soul that our culture fosters.

I'd like to turn our attention to a view of psychosis that existed in earlier cultures. This view is reemerging in psychiatric thinkers such as R. D. Laing, who saw psychosis as a natural way of healing our own appalling state of alienation called normality. He saw, as did earlier cultures, that the psychotic individual could be recognized as a hierophant of the sacred. This is a view that sees psychosis as a vital and positive opportunity to awaken to our deeper motives for incarnation. Stanislav and Christina Grof, founders of the Spiritual Emergence Network, have developed a way of working with those in psychosis. It is aimed at guiding them to become more aware of their pre-earthly intentions—a work worthy of our calling. Yet only one who has crossed the threshold of the spiritual world can have the wisdom to guide or accompany another through it. And this must be learned, for not every psychotherapist is an elder shaman. The task before us is much larger than this. It involves a whole culture that is in psychosis.

Traditions of an initiation process were built into ancient cultures, but these have been lost to most of Western civilization. Our inability to create such rites of passage and other events to mark turning points in life has left a vacuum. Perversions of the initiation process now take their place, and in some cases, a kind of dark initiation into evil is taking place. Such perversions are to be seen in our modern pathologies.

I will illustrate this by utilizing the framework of a Native American initiation process. We are acquainted with it primarily through the idea of the vision quest, which is often a rite of passage for adolescents who are about to receive their second birth—the birth of their soul.

The first stage is a preparation by purification, which commonly includes the sweat lodge and fasting. One prepares for the quest by becoming naked and praying and by working with the basic instincts of the body through exercise and rest. We find remnants of this in our culture as the pathology of anorexia and bulimia and as a variety

of sexual disorders and perversions. Within these phenomena, there is a common factor of fear—either the fear
of touching the world or the fear of not being able to be
touched by the world. There is an urge to take flight from
the body, to excarnate. This arises from a soul that feels
trapped in the body and dominated by instincts. If not
consciously embraced and guided to a higher service, the
instinctual life becomes compulsions in the soul.

The second stage of the initiation process is the art of
learning to truly perceive nature as a living organism, of
which we are a part. It is a way of learning to breathe in
sensory perceptions as a gift of the divine—the spirit at
work in nature. At this stage, the adolescent or adult
would go into nature alone for three days. This, too, has
fallen into pathologies of a neurotic disorder. Overstimu-
lation of sensory impressions and excitement flood the
soul life, leaving one helpless to dissolve images and turn
them into meaningful experiences. The result is nervous
anxiety. The inability to find nature in our synthetic, tech-
nological environment often gives rise to a tendency to
indulge in dream, fantasy, and wishes that can rarely be
fulfilled. A certain mania of restless activity is all too
common in our culture. In this stage of the perverted initiation process, the soul breathing is disturbed, and the
soul is dominated by unconscious drives stimulated by
the environment. It manifests as a fear of being detached
from the environment of technology, hence a fear of
nature or a fear of the environment altogether.

In the third stage of the initiation process, one culti-
vates the capacity to distinguish the essential from the
nonessential, the necessary from the unnecessary,
through a life of simplicity. Living alone in the woods or
the desert, the person learned how to live with nature, to
eradicate desires that could not be fulfilled, and to
develop skills to meet the needs of people. All of this has
been perverted in our culture by images of a fantastic,

unreal nature that splits our soul life into images and desires that often have nothing to do with who we are. The inability to discern our needs and the lack of self-reliance to meet our needs creates deep soul frustration. The complexity of life overwhelms and diffuses the soul forces into a state of meaninglessness. Many types of schizophrenia and psychotic illnesses have their origin in this set of experiences. Many turn to drugs or other forms of addictions to escape the meaninglessness of the culture. In these situations, the soul is dominated by desires that find no fulfillment. It is like living in purgatory.

The fourth stage of the initiation process is the search for and discovery of one's vision. This has a special character from the other side of the threshold. It is the ideal intention for one's life and reveals one's destiny. In our culture, this stage is hindered by the pursuit of happiness, which is often characterized by the popular dogma of materialism or by the new age slogan "be happy." The image of what it means to be human is distorted in many ways. The constant engagement in false pursuits—the anti-life—leaves the soul little time for silence and contemplation, which are needed for acquiring a vision of one's destiny. The soul is led by a regressive tendency to expect and follow images presented from without by authority figures. This is what took place in former times when the soul still retained a natural clairvoyance, and priests were able to convey images from the spiritual world. At that time, this was a proper way to be led into the spiritual world. Today it is no longer right. It not only offends the souls longing for freedom, but can become a form of manipulation to control others; hence it can become a form of evil. Today this tendency only breaks down the soul's capacity for self-judgment and initiative.

Returning from the quest, which is the fifth stage, the individual was given a warm reception by fellow brothers and sisters. Within this circle of embrace, the person articulated the vision and resolved to carry it out. Everyone in the tribe or community felt a responsibility to hold the individual accountable to fulfilling the vision. Such accountability was both an acceptance of the vision bearer as a full human being and the recognition that a true human community acts responsibly and provides an initiation process for all its members. Because our culture lacks this sense of the vision quest and this accountability, we instead provide space for social pathologies, whereby the rage of the soul is not recognized but acted out through aggression and war.

The sixth stage in this process was a celebration of the mysteries of life. It included the sacrament of song, dance, and arts that affirmed reverence for life. The social contract was in this celebration, in which the vision bearer would agree to abide by the laws and customs of the tribe. It was an expression of gratitude for all that one was given. In our culture, there are few opportunities to consciously honor our social contract or express gratitude. The sacred has become secular, pervaded by irreverence and lack of respect for life. I ask you, is this not a social pathology? Does this not enforce conditions for psychosis?

Finally, the seventh stage involves an act of remembrance initiated by the vision bearer, who vows to the Great Spirit to "walk the talk" and to live a life of integrity, which means simply that the vision bearer would strive to be as fully human as possible, so that others could do the same. In our culture we experience disintegrity. It is a culture of self-centeredness, a culture in which this attitude has led to a sense of complete disintegration of culture.

As we strive toward a human psychosophy, we must keep in mind, equally, both the individual soul and the life of our whole culture. We are in a momentous time. The Sophia is being threatened by the Dragon of our own creations. We must stand by the side of Michael and wield the sword that is ours to wield.

I call upon you to do this here and now. It is my three-fold wish that, first, we have the resolve to disseminate the ideal image of the human being ensouled with Anthrophsophia; second, that we aspire to the highest in us and give birth to our Spirit Self on a daily basis by taking ownership of our incompleteness, our karma, our destiny; and third, that we create a movement worthy of the integrity of what has been given to us by Anthroposophia—that we do this for the sake of healing the World Soul.

It is the wisdom of the true nature of the human soul that must be disseminated into the mainstream of our culture. To do this, we have to find the loving collegiality to hold one another accountable to being the highest we can be, and to affirm the individual sense of destiny of one another. Out of such collegiality, we may create a movement wherein psychosophy can be seen as a path which introduces the seven conditions of esoteric training into the main institutions of our culture.[6]

---

6. See Rudolf Steiner, *How To Know Higher Worlds.*

5. The Human Heart: Source and Substance of The Holy Grail

Everything about the human heart pervades our lives. It lives in our language in so many ways. The word _heart_ has come to mean the portal of understanding of our soul life. In each language, there is a way in which poets and those who are involved in the art of shaping and crafting the word use the heart as a central motif. I will begin with a poem by Edna St. Vincent Millay, which points toward the wide dimension that we will explore here:

> The world stands out on either side
> No wider than the heart is wide.
> Above the world is stretched the sky
> No higher than the soul is high.
> The heart can push the sea and land
> Farther away on either hand.
> The soul can split the sky in two
> And let the face of God shine through.
> But East and West will pinch that heart
> That cannot keep them held apart.
> And he whose soul is flat—the sky
> Will cave in on him by and by.

We also find wonderful treasures if we look into the Holy Book on the question of the heart. I would like to build this talk fundamentally on one sentence, which is found in Matthew 12:34. It is a rather simple statement, yet as I started to pivot my ideas and thoughts around it, I realized how much it opened up. It is simply this: "For out of the abundance of the heart the mouth speaketh." Let us ask, What is the abundance of the heart? From whence does it come? And how does it flow through the mouth as speech? These questions can certainly be taken up as meditative content.

There can be no dispute that the heart is the most central organ in the human being. There are many reasons we can put forward to substantiate this, which I will not go into here. I would, however, like to mention perhaps the central reason why the heart is most important—that is, the realization that the heart is the source of life, health, and all the attributes that we ascribe to the nature of goodness. Goodness is the distinctive quality that each human being continually strives to become. To become good has a great deal to do with a purity and a magnanimity of the heart. It is not so hard to see that this abundance of life is all around us. It's in nature. We see it in the cycles of vegetation and wherever we see birth, life, death, and rebirth. The goddess Natura herself mirrors to us the genius in the mystery of life around us and speaks to us the same truth; for all life on Earth, animal life as well as the human being, also undergoes birth, life, death and rebirth. The heart knows this.

Life is given to us and given to us in abundance. But what is not given to us is the underlying connection between life on the Earth and the wonderful ongoing tapestry of the heavens. In this there is a glorious counterpart to Natura—a heavenly Sophia, who enfolds us in the wide sky with an embrace that you might say is as tender and dear as mother to child.

How are we nourished by this? How are we to understand this intimate connection between our life on the Earth and in the heavens? It is something we must give thoughtful attention to. Only in this way can we answer fully from whence this abundance comes. We know that it would be rather narrow to believe this abundance comes only from beneath our feet, out of the earth as a kind of cause and effect situation. To accept this limited idea would be to fall into a materialistic concept. We must stretch ourselves and develop a trans-rational understanding based on the hermetic axiom "as above, so below." If we take this as a way to reorient our attention and to see the corresponding phenomena of earthly and heavenly life, we begin to see that poetic phrases reflect cosmic facts when describing the heart as the human seat of warmth, light, and even levity. Human movement comes through the grace and tact of the heart, which reflects a deeper sense of intentionality than the mere appearance of movement. Within the heart is the seat of the ego being who orients all movement in accordance with a divine plan, forming character at the core of its being.

All of these characterizations are equally true for the Sun, which lies there in the center of our solar system, radiating warmth and light. In this wonderful, choreo-graphed dance between the Earth and the Sun, we have the circulation of this warmth and light. Consequently, there is a movement that conveys a sense of point and periphery, an understanding between the Sun and the Earth that is complementary. Indeed, on one hand, the Sun is the center, and around it the Earth moves; and yet, on the other hand, this point and periphery is a marvel-ous mystery, for we can also state that the Earth is the point, and the Sun is moving in the periphery. This is a perceptible, phenomenal experience.

If we bring thoughtful attention to it, we begin to fol-low this relationship between Sun and Earth and find that the relationship is actually between the Sun and the human heart. In our human organism, we attempt to come to this balance point of a breath–pulse ratio of one to four. This ratio of four pulses to one breath can be understood when we follow it through as something that mirrors the entire movement of the heavens. Each minute we take eighteen breaths, on average, compared to seventy-two pulses of the blood. Seventy-two is a number of mystery in itself. Seventy-two years is the length of time it takes the vernal point to move one full degree in the background of the zodiac.[1] Following the breath cycle through the day, we find that, if we multiply sixty times eighteen breaths for an hour, and multiply it by twenty-four hours, we come up with twenty-five thousand, nine hundred and twenty breaths. That is the number of years it takes for the vernal point to make one complete circle around the zodiac.

And so it is no surprise to us when the spiritual traditions of both East and West tell us that the mystery of the heart has to do with a twelvefold radiation, or a twelve-petalled lotus. It is mirroring the Sun in its twelvefold streaming out into the zodiac. There is also a microcosmic world that has condensed into the very center of the human being. It lives as the heart. This ordering—this wonderful ratio of breath and pulse—shows us that the heart has a great deal to do with the maintenance of health. If the heart grows tired and stops or lags behind, one becomes ill or dies. That is how vital the heart is to our sense of health. But if we were to stop at this point, we would not really enter into this question of what is so distinct about the human being. From whence comes this striving to be good? From whence comes this moral template that every human being attempts to embody?

---

1. Vernal point is the moment in the cycle of the year wherein day and night are equal in length during the spring season. It is at present March twenty-one. Every seventy-two years this point will have moved one full degree in relation to the zodiac. Today it is in the sixth degree of the Fishes; hence we are in the astrological age of Pisces.

Imagine that abundance is really the result of a resolution of the Holy Trinity. Within the Holy Trinity there was a resolve to impart a form of evolution which would have abundance. This resolve was given a certain guiding intention by the Seraphim, the Spirits of Love, who fell in love with the resolve for abundance and wished that love would become abundant in this creative process. This was then taken up by the Cherubim, who had a powerful sense of wish. Their wish lived in an ordering Imagination, which has an intrinsic order, an intrinsic architecture that manifests itself. This can be understood as the basis of magic. The Cherubim then created what we now know as the zodiac, which helped bring order into this creation and within which harmony was to work. The harmony has always been the intimate link between the moral resolve of the Trinity and that which shines through the zodiac.

All of this was received by the Thrones. The Thrones, or Spirits of Will, received it, affirmed it, and made it their motive for creating the evolutionary process that we refer to as ancient Saturn. The Spirits of Will became completely devoted to this resolve, intention, and Imagination. Through sacrifice, their motive became the signature of the whole process of human evolution. Their devotion became such a power of sacrifice that the first flow of divine creation existed as pure warmth. Warmth begets warmth begets warmth, and ancient Sun became the origin of the heart. As it has manifested in the human being, we cannot think of the heart without the blood's circulation. In that respect, it is something that begins to emerge archetypally in the ancient Sun. But I would say that the heart was there even earlier, as warmth, in ancient Saturn. It was there as an idea of the gods. This warmth, which was held by the upper gods' tremendous interest and attention, became the seed for abundance. This is the warmth that flowed into the creation of the heart. Today it is still remembered in the zodiac as a shining image in the constellation of the Lion. The tremendous blue, vibrant, first-magnitude star Regulus is the heart of the Lion. Rudolf Steiner says that the memory of ancient Saturn is in this star.

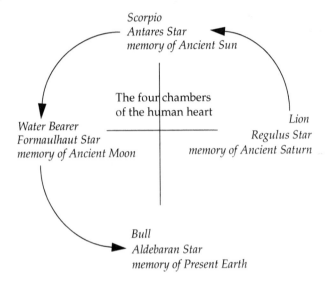

Scorpio
Antares Star
memory of Ancient Sun

The four chambers
of the human heart

Water Bearer
Formaulhaut Star
memory of Ancient Moon

Lion
Regulus Star
memory of Ancient Saturn

Bull
Aldebaran Star
memory of Present Earth

Even ancient Arabian astrologers had an intimation of this. They called this star Regulus, because they believed the whole cosmos was regulated by the heart of the Lion. This whole constellation of the Lion is imprinted in the human being within the heart. It gives us a spiritualized basis for understanding the heart and its primary importance in us. The ancient Sun gives us a picture of what can truly become heart. The ancient Sun is all about the mystery of light; and this light begets life. The great heart-star Antares is in the constellation of the Scorpion, the portal of the mysteries of life and death.

Following warmth in ancient Saturn and light in ancient Sun, with the ancient Moon we come to movement. That light that began to pulsate, radiate, and stream out in the Ancient Sun begins to interact with the movement of darkness. One might say that this movement of darkness is where the fall of Lucifer took place. With this event, the purity of our astral body was lost. This fall from the ability to maintain a right relationship to the moral forces streaming out of the zodiac gives birth to the fallen astral body, which is especially represented by the asteroid belt. This is remembered in the constellation of Aquarius, the Waterman and the age we are moving toward.

During this age, we must redeem the astral body through soul purification. In the fixed star called Fomaulhaut, the Water Bearer is pouring new life out of his urn into the mouth of the southern fish. Here we see an imagination of the streaming of the blood, which can become the quickening of new life. Now the blood no longer merely pulsates; in the ancient Moon it began to circulate in an ordered, rhythmic movement, as do the planets in our solar system.

Finally, we come to the present Earth phase of cosmic evolution. The Earth is a globe—not so much of warmth and light and movement alone, but all that has taken on visible, manifest form. This whole evolution is formed and imprinted in the heart. We see this remembered in the constellation of the Bull, where we find the fixed star Aldebaran, called the eye of the Bull. In the zodiac, it is exactly 180 degrees from the fixed star Antares. There is an axis in the cosmos between the ancient Sun and the present Earth. If we follow the other axis, from the Lion to the Water Bearer, we have this tremendous cross in the heavens. This cross is mirrored in the four chambers of the heart. It is also mirrored in the fact that the Earth—which has to form a right relationship to the Sun's warmth, light, and circulation—is tilted on its axis; similarly, our heart tilts on its axis. Here are wonderful correlations and associations between the mystery of the heart and the cosmos. But we can go further, particularly if we look for the origin of the human heart.

Let us take a moment to look at just one detailed aspect of embryology. The inner organs exist not only in space but in time; their developmental process mirrors time. And because the time process of the world is part of this development, it is condensed in place spatially, so that we can see time in space. Think of this: we can actually perceive time in space. We perceive it by seeing life in its development and in its metamorphic forms. In embryology, it is a very dynamic experience to see how life develops with all its metamorphic forms. Between the skull and the brain there is a lining of membranes. And between these membranes there is a fluid we call the cerebrospinal fluid. It is upon this fluid that the brain is able to float, actually displacing its weight of about 1500 grams into about twenty grams. So even in the cerebrospinal fluid we find the mystery of levity. In the whole formation of the brain, we have a certain soft lining that covers the head. For the first three weeks it is like a cap. The starry configuration that took place at conception is imprinted around the head during these first three weeks. This imprint becomes a living force that will work down from the brain, influencing the whole embryonic development. The brain becomes a mirror through which the soul will continually receive its pre-earthly intentions. This force of levity begins to take place shortly after the first three weeks. The pericardial sinus starts to separate from the head, feels the forces of gravitation, and moves down on the stream of the fluids to become the pericardial sac, where all the blood vessels are. It is these vessels that are really the source of the heart. It moves down into the chest cavity and takes its place as a kind of chalice, and this becomes the foundation for the heart. Here we have a gesture of what will become a mirror for the soul life streaming in. The ego organization slips into the fluid stream and goes into this middle sphere, where the ego being will dwell in the heart.

This phenomenon is also mirrored in the cosmos. We can now make our analogy; the heart equals the Sun and vice versa. The Sun streams down, and as it does so the light streams into the Moon sphere. At night we see how the Moon takes the light of the Sun and beams it down to Earth. But the Moon doesn't remain stationary. It also circulates around the Earth. In a certain way, imaginations resolved by the highest gods flow from the astral world (the world of stars) and enter the Sun as moral substance. And sunlight gives moral substance to human beings by shining down into the Earth. This substance also passes into the Moon, which can be felt and experienced as the place where we find the names of those seeking the Grail.

This is a Grail image. In that sense I would say that the heart bears a great relationship to the Grail, for it has the same source and eventually becomes the very same substance.

Now, in the beginning, the heart was a sense organ. This fact takes us all the way back to ancient Saturn. The heart was a sense organ for the touch of God. Even today, we have certain remembrances, or echoes, that the human being is "touched" into existence. Think of Michaelangelo's great painting of Creation in the Sistine Chapel. This touch from the gods creates a sensation of warmth. In the quiet of our prayers and meditations, when we have been touched by the presence of a spiritual world, we experience inwardly a deep sense of warmth. This is a phenomenon and an occult fact. So the heart was initially a sense organ for the touch of the spirit, and the sensation of that touching was warmth.

The real task behind the Holy Grail—one that concerns us implicitly in the development of the heart—is to restore the heart to a sense organ. It is not merely an organ for circulation and certainly not to be perceived as a "pump." When we crack open the deepest mysteries and secrets of the heart, it will have to do with the embodiment of the Holy Grail within us. This is the great work. It is something we must learn to do in our time. Earth evolution was given its inaugural formation through the Exusiai, the Spirits of Form, who carry the impulse for the I AM. This impulse of the ego finds its proper dwelling place upon the throne within the heart. This I AM works even in the embryonic stages of the blood circulation. During the first moments of conception, the ego forces work to maintain that conception until the placenta has formed. It does so by sending blood circulation into the uterus in a very particular way, already containing the seeds of the ego formation in its warmth.

Now we come to a certain connection between the great cosmic starry world and the human spark of divinity, the I AM. It is from the cosmos that the I AM visits the Earth in a temple we call the human body. Through this body, the I AM attempts to generate new life for future evolution. We have seen how, at conception, the starry world imprints into the malleable template of the brain its imaginations of our resolves and intentions to become good. To become good is merely to become a servant of God. Each of us must serve in a particular way. We all have a task that is imprinted upon the brain, not at conception but at birth. This imprinting awaits an awakening. The force for that awakening comes not so much from the brain, but from the dwelling of the ego. It is the force of the starry configuration at conception that slipped into the heart with the pericardial sac. These pre-earthly intentions begin to radiate in the heart at puberty. So strong is this call to become oneself that all the etheric encasing of the heart cracks open. The stars of one's birth shine into the heart and a new heart is formed. This gesture recapitulates what occurred at three weeks in the embryo; a chalice is formed for the reception of one's karma and destiny. We have a second birth at that point in adolescence. It is the birth of accountability to one's karma. And so adolescents indeed undergo a death. They seek their rebirth by trying to find other human beings who have had the courage to pursue their ideals.

There is also a third birth yet to come. But once we have set out on our quest to become as good as we can be—to embody the ideals that we have resolved to bring—we will have to become co-creators of this evolutionary process. We will have to develop a power that was present in the beginning: the Word, speech, the Logos. Our speech must have the same creative power as the entire cosmos. In the search for the Holy Grail, we are attempting to lift the chalice of the heart so that its contents will flow from our mouths. This is the third birth, whereby all that overflows from the heart will go through the larynx and then flow from the mouth. In this process, the mouth will speak from the abundance of the heart. It will speak with incredible creative forces.

This points to a physiosophy, intimated by the fact that the tongue is an important object of diagnoses for the heart. If it is purplish, we know that the heart and the blood circulation are racing almost aggressively. If it is white and pale, circulation is too slow. So we see that there is an intimate relationship physiologically between the mouth and the heart. In a certain sense, we can now say that the mystery of the soul senses becomes important. Rudolf Steiner describes twelve senses. The four lower ones are senses of touch, life, movement, and balance. The middle senses, which we are concerned with, have to do with smell and taste, sight, and warmth. The mouth is the portal through which we receive nourishment into ourselves from the earth. Often smell is very intimately connected with taste. The mouth does not have four chambers, as does the heart, but it perceives four tastes: sweet, salty, sour, and bitter. And, just as we taste the substances we take into the mouth, the heart tastes the quality of the blood. We see here the two senses of smell and taste. There are also the soul senses that have to do with sight and warmth. Now we are back where we began—with warmth. In the future, people may come to understand more deeply that these senses of sight and warmth are not related to meeting the solid substances of the Earth, but to meeting the life-quickening ethers of the Earth.

People will soon recognize the difference between viewing violence on television and viewing a bird on a tree. The difference is the qualitative impact. We can discover that qualitative impact by determining whether we are warmed more by watching violence in a cinema or by watching a bird in a tree. Lift this into an understanding of speech, for speech can also create images. Images behind words can either warm or freeze. What occurs in the mouth is really a metamorphosis of events in the heart. The principal difference is inversion, or the fundamental architectural law of how human beings move from one incarnation to the next. Events in the four chambers of the heart are metamorphosed and turned outward. They are turned outward in the mouth by the tongue. So a new cavity arises, which is the mouth, and that tireless muscle of the heart metamorphoses and becomes the tongue. The tongue has no chambers, but the tongue creates and forms chambers. The tongue moves quickly, opening and closing the air passages so that we can utter sounds as vowels and consonants. Without the tongue we would not be able to articulate speech. Think of how the tongue is given to us from the heart of the previous incarnation. How marvelous an imagination to behold.

For animals, the mouth and tongue primarily serve in the nourishment process of earth substances. But for the human being, it serves to pour out spiritual nourishment.

And that is what the word can be. The mouth wills to pour out spiritual nourishment. "From out of the abundance of the heart the mouth speaketh."

Let us continue with the quote that we find in Matthew 12:34–35. "A good man, out of the good treasures of the heart, bringeth forth good things. An evil man, out of the evil treasures, brings forth evil things." We come now to this third theme about goodness and its relationship to the mystery of speech. If we look into the inmost workings of the heart, we realize that the heart is intimately connected with the system of metabolism and the limbs. These forces stream in through the blood from the metabolic system and the limbs. The heart tastes it, listens to it, and perceives the quality of our deeds. For the most part, the heart is quiet because it is a "listening" organ for the karma being created by the human being. It weighs it up and asks, "What is the moral value of these deeds?"

In the next incarnation, what the heart remembers as deeds done or not done will be poured out into the world to be met from outside as one's destiny, and the deeper consequences of destiny usually arise as obstacles. The tongue must form obstructions in the airflow if we are to speak, and the heart does the same thing for us. It creates obstacles so that we can meet our destiny. But since the advent of the incarnation of Christ, the heart no longer wishes to be silent but is beginning to speak, and it speaks through the phenomenon of conscience. Here the heart is not just tasting, perceiving, and experiencing karma; the heart hears the flow of time from the future into the present. That is conscience.

So the real task of the heart is to become a sense organ for time. It is the Grail mystery. How can time be perceived as a spatial tableau that contains the whole mystery of the unfolding soul? And how do we develop this more consciously? We might say that it is the heart, as a sense organ, that actually perceives karma. The sense organ of the heart hears destiny. When these aspects are awakened, the heart becomes a source of knowing through feeling. This hearing is the basis of the higher senses. Only when it is active can we speak the word with thoughts of the I AM. The heart is the place that comprehends the truth of one's own existence. That's why, when conscience speaks, it is undeniable; it never lies. Conscience is always true. However, we often lack the courage to abide by it. And when we don't abide by it, we are being disobedient to God.

Inwardly, we must come to this third new birth of the cosmos within us. We must bring the abundance of the heart into speech, and that is a meditative activity. In this meditative activity, the natural processes of breaking down blood cells and freeing our ether forces to nourish the soul life must become more conscious. We already have a normative process of this. If we look for the organ within the brain that performs these functions, we are led to the pineal gland. It is involved in the etherization of the blood. This is a natural process that takes place within the pineal gland.

The pineal gland secretes a kind of granular "sand." The biochemistry has to do with myocardium, something you can find in only two other places in the organism—the heart and the tongue. The third place is the pineal gland. It secretes a kind of fine crystal that contributes to the activity of the eyes. It aids the function and crystalline structure of seeing. But seeing is given to us, so it is not a process we need to work on. To see the sense-perceptible world is a gift of the upper gods. But what about the ability to see the supersensible worlds that exist behind form? This is why we take up the practice of meditation. Meditative attentiveness to the moral content of thought—whether it is the Rose Cross or a mantra—enters the blood stream and frees the ether forces attached to our organs.[2] We begin to create a power of levity. By freeing up ether forces, a life process takes place in the soul. Meditation brings something that is capable of engendering an etherization of the blood. When you meditate, the soul takes in the object of that meditation by breathing it in. We breathe in this content that has an affinity to divine thought, so we breathe in divine thoughts. There was a time in human evolution when, in the East, rhythmic, tantric breathing was really enhanced thinking. I am not talking about physiological breathing, however, but soul breathing—a new yoga of taking in divine thoughts. When we do that in meditation, this life process immediately becomes warmth within us. If we have been attentive, this warmth gives us an experience of discernment. We begin to discern and grasp the essence of the moral content of meditation. By touching what is given by the spiritual beings, there is warmth. This warmth becomes a fire in the blood, which releases the ethers and sends it upward as nourishment. In our meditation, the image becomes the essence of our meditative content, which accompanies the etherization of the blood and separates it from the actual object of meditation. When we build up the rose cross in meditation, we know there is a point at which we must let go of the imagined form, while the essence of the color and light of that image separates from the form and begins to etherize the blood. Thus, the soul is nourished by the essence of divinity as living images ride up to the head on waves of etherized blood. This essence of divinity meets the pineal gland and creates a spiritualized secretion of granular sands. This granular substance, this myocardium, has an affinity to the myocardium in the heart. It is as though a piece of the heart is moved into the pineal gland and from there into the pituitary.

---

2. The Rose Cross meditation is described by Rudolf Steiner in *An Outline of Esoteric Science*, pp. 289–295.

The pituitary is a concave organ within the brow of the forehead; it receives this piece of the heart, which contains an essence of morality and is filled with light. The pituitary is able to sustain this higher knowledge, because within the pituitary gland the essence of morality is connected to our own life. We individualize what we have taken in as meditative content—not merely as a wisdom that we have been able to grasp from ancient knowledge, but as a wisdom of our own life. This piece of wisdom acts as a kind of swelling within the pituitary gland.

The next process in the etherization of the blood takes place when the pituitary grows and, by swelling, opens the third eye. We now begin to see our Spirit Self. It is this vision of Spirit Self that is the Grail. We begin to see how we are perceived by spiritual beings, for any genuine meditative experience is not a one-way seeing. When you are within the silence, you have an experience of presence, and you are perceived in a meeting between you and the bearers of this spiritualized, divine thought that you have made your own. In this moment you are a part of the Gods. And because you have crossed the threshold of the spiritual world in this way, you have an implicit mandate to cross back and become creative, just as the Gods have been.

The last life process in the soul is to reproduce the divine thoughts in deed. This light of etherized blood must flow down from the pituitary and come into the mouth and the tongue, wherein the most creative human act takes place. Out of speech we create our social reality. The great physician Paracelsus said, "Speech is not of the tongue, but of the heart. The tongue is merely the instrument of speech." Consider this remarkable power of the Logos. For one moment think of the words that were spoken by the Christ. His words nourished the souls of human beings. The way in which he spoke healed human

'tongues of fire'

beings. His command of speech initiated human beings. The Christ bore the heart of the future. This heart of the future is not only where the ego dwells and senses karma; it is where the "Not I, but Christ in me" dwells. Speaking as your voice of conscience, the "Not I but Christ in me" speaks to me—only to me—about my karma and my destiny. No one else can hear that private conversation in one's heart. Out of that, I am guided to the aims of my incarnation.

The heart of the future knows not only the source of the Holy Grail, but will become the substance of the Holy Grail. In our time we know that all around there is increasing heart failure, physically, psychologically, and indeed spiritually. The heart can fail. The great struggle in one's heart can contain elements of a pervasive pathology. And behind it lies the great fear that we will fail to fulfill our destiny. This is the spiritual battle within every soul.

We live in the time of the consciousness soul, which means we live in a time when the human being must spiritualize the soul. In this period of the consciousness soul, through the resolve and the intentions of higher beings we know that this will be the time when the etheric body will be loosened. It takes place in stages. The Archangel Gabriel worked from 1529 until about 1879. It was Gabriel's task to lift the etheric forces slightly higher from the head organism. This brought with it both gifts and hindrances. On the one hand, it allowed the new capacity of Imagination, which has permeated human-kind from the time of the Renaissance forward. That was the gift. We were given the gift of Imagination. The hin-drances, on the other hand, left the brain more gravity bound, more interested in substance and earth, and more forgetful of the imprint of the cosmos upon the brain. This situation has fallen into mere intellectuality. In this intellectuality, we have forgotten the heavenly template that the stars imprinted upon the image of the human being. We have, in essence, forgotten the image of the human being. Instead we have an excessive drive to become the invincible animal-machine.

In 1879 the age of the Archangel Michael dawned. It will last until 2229. In this age, the etheric forces are loosening from the heart. In this process there is a gift from Michael. There are also counter forces to it. The gift Michael wishes to give goes beyond the capacity for Imagination; it is the capacity for Inspiration. In this context, Inspiration is the embodiment of divine thought in human speech. Michael's sword lies within our own mouths as our tongue. It is the sword we wield in the world. It can wound or it can heal, and it must experience the fire of inspiration pouring down if it is to heal.The hindrance in the Michael Age, as the ethers separate from the substance of the heart, is that human beings no longer know how to speak to one another. We have become isolated. In our isolation, we increasingly lack the capacity for intimacy. Truthful words invite intimacy; untruth creates distance. With this isolation comes a deeper sense of alienation from our brothers and sisters. We are losing the heart for relationships.

In the future, as the Archangel Orphiel takes hold in the twenty-third century, there will be a loosening from the metabolic and limb system. In a certain way, that is what we are preparing for. When this occurs, the human being will gain the capacity to embody others through the power of love. It will become Intuition. Right now the danger is to become separated at the heart level, so there is no willingness to stream into the other with love. What we have in our time, already working out of the future, is a kind of dark side of the Orphielic reign. This hindrance is insensitivity. We have forgotten the image of the human being. We no longer know how to relate with one another. Therefore it becomes easier and easier for us to view each other as objects we can manipulate, just as we

would any other substance in the world. This insensitivity is completely devoid of creativity. It has within it an
underlying sense of destruction and rage.

These are part of the pathologies of our time. They
have to do with the battle for the open space within the
heart. The danger is that this free space of the heart—
where the warmth substance and the warmth ether
remain together—may be separated. This altar in the
heart, where the flame of offering is found, is vulnerable.
Circulating through the heart as blood is the Hermes'
staff of the physician. But the flame of offering and Hermes' staff are equally in danger of attack. Our anthroposophical doctors know this and need continually to
connect the heavenly forces with the substances of the
earth as a healing path. As healers, we need to take up the
path of offering and pastoral care. We must tend the
flame and continue to bring the moral substance of the
cosmos into our speech every day, every time we tend to
another. And in attempting to do this, we will experience
the battle for the soul. It is in our culture.

We have a powerful cultural double that we have to
fight, day in and day out. This cultural double is the creation of the three beasts. It has infected our culture in
such a way that young people fear the world. They have a
certain sense of self-hate, which usually develops into an
inability to love another; therefore they hate the other. A
pervasive sense of doubt that the spiritual world exists is
all too prevalent in today's education.

We think of these things, and to some extent we can
bear them. But it is quickly becoming unbearable. When
we talk about humanity crossing the threshold of the
spiritual world, we mean all of humanity, including the
infant born today. Infants are also surrounded by the cultural double, and it will eventually have an impact. The
pathology that will seat itself in the heart, which I would
say is most characteristic, has to do with trauma and

abuse at all levels: physical, emotional, sexual, and psychological. This archetypal trauma and abuse lies in the realization that we no longer can be assured of finding the light of spiritual and divine archetypes in nature and human beings. Often we find this double, this lie, where no truth for the heart can be found. And that in itself is trauma and can lead to an aborted quest for the Holy Grail.

There are three psychological mechanisms that are the outcome of being touched by the cultural double—of having experienced, on some level at some point in time, trauma and abuse. The first is compartmentalization. This is a method many of us have learned to use in coping with our lives. We put this activity and that situation over here and keep it separate from anything else we may do or be involved with in life. We compartmentalize our experiences, our feelings, and our thoughts, and in that sense we live only in the present situation given to us. Compartmentalizing assures us that there is no past and no future. Just think of this—there is no past and there is no future. We become fixed in the present situation. This is the triumph of Ahriman, who is then able to harden the etheric body and prevent any etherization of the blood.

This can go a level deeper when compartmentalization, at some point or other, is accompanied by exposure to the cultural double. Trauma and abuse can strike so deep that it becomes dissociation. We are all aware that, in the last couple of decades, there was a pathology called multiple personality disorder, whereby individuals had subsets of personalities living in them. This became so sensationalized that people actually joked about it. It is not a joking matter. At least the American Psychiatric Association realized it is not a joking matter, because it is no longer considered a personality disorder. They now call it a dissociation identity disorder, a major psychotic experience.

It is a reality that many, many people are experiencing dissociation from life, which means they have no sense of time. They live in an excarnated space with the unborn, the dead, and all the specters and phantoms that are living as unfinished karma around us. Think of living in that space. Because Ahriman has been able to push the soul out, he can invite various elemental and demonic beings to inhabit the human being. This is possession—an occult fact that takes place on a wider scale than we wish to acknowledge.

Imagine being in that space and still having your heartbeat—still having your heart perceive all the paralyzed attempts to meet your destiny. Eventually there is only one course for somebody who experiences this in the heart. Such despair leads to suicidal ideation. "Let me finish it now before it gets worse." Ahriman is then able to steal the unused ether forces and use them from the other side of the threshold to disempower us. All of this is aimed at preventing us from fulfilling our destiny.

Those of us who want to take up the work of a pastoral care and wish to wed psychosophy with physiosophy have a mighty task ahead. We must all become Grail Knights of the Word. We have to forge an iron sword of courage in our hearts. Courage is the warmth substance of the heart. Courage is the throne upon which the ego should sit. We've got to assume our rightful throne in our own hearts and light the way for our brothers and sisters who also seek the Holy Grail. We must do this for our brothers and sisters, because not one of us will ever go to the inner sanctum of the Holy Grail alone; we have to take someone with us. We have to love someone so deeply that the other will be transformed. We have to take on the work of the spiritual hierarchies, who are being obscured and denied direct access to us by the counterforces of our time. The Holy Grail is all about the mystery of the battle between good and evil. There is no room for contentment or a lukewarm heart. According to a correct understanding of the Apocalypse, lukewarm is unacceptable. The heart must be completely transformed into a shining inner Sun. The heart that is good must be the heart that burns with the flame of offering.

We are asked to step into this world of pastoral care and to realize that the only way we can counter these three pathological forces is to enter deeply into the mysteries of physiosophy. Physiosophy, the mystery of the cosmic forces embedded in the substance of earth and the human organism, can give us renewed faith in the powers of the spiritual world. They do work. They wait only for us to understand so that we can ally ourselves with their activity. It is a deep mystery, one that concerns the building of the temple. We have to enkindle faith in the power of the spirit. We must learn to love our incarnation with all its struggles and obstacles, and we must teach others to do the same. We can teach others to love their incarnations only when we can absolutely speak with enthusiasm of how much we love our own.

When you seek to be a Grail Knight, you must be willing to sacrifice aspects of your personal life for the devotion of serving the gods. In this service there is another type of joy. It is a joy that can be regarded as bliss, as divine fulfillment. In the realm of psychosophy, our task is to teach others to love their own incarnation—not to hate or fear it, but to love it. Eventually we will need to develop something new, something that has been called sociosophy. We know we cannot heal or turn the tide of the events of this world unless we meet this cultural double with a new sense of what it means to be fully social. Without this, the human being is not complete. To become fully social beings we must create, through our speech and deeds with one another, living ideals capable of refashioning the world we live in. In this way, we will be able to bring hope as we create a new world.

These are the tasks that lie before us. Anything less will not do. Our life is all about striving to do the Good. We all know that, on a daily basis, we fail to be perfectly good, but knowing this makes us human. Waking up the next morning and attempting again to do the Good brings us closer to divinity. Carry this in your hearts.

BIBLIOGRAPHY & FURTHER READING

American Psychiatric Association, *Diagnostic and Statistical Manual of Mental Disorders: DSM-IV-TR*, 4th ed., text revision, Washington, DC: American Psychiatric Association, 2000.

Ben-Aharon, Jesaiah, *The New Experience of the Supersensible*, London: Temple Lodge, 1995.

Breggin, Peter R., *Talking Back to Prozac: What Doctors Aren't Telling You About Today's Most Controversial Drug*, New York: St. Martin's Press, 1994.

Dyson, James A., *Initiation or Aberration? The Physiology and Diagnosis of Mental Illness*, Great Barrington, MA: SteinerBooks, 2003.

Kühlewind, Georg, *From Normal to Healthy: Paths to the Liberation of Consciousness*, Great Barrington, MA: Lindisfarne Books, 1988.

———, *The Life of the Soul: Between Subconsciousness and Supraconsciousness*, Great Barrington, MA: Lindisfarne Books, 1990.

———, *Meditation for the Soft Will*, Great Barrington, MA: Lindisfarne Books, 2003.

———, *Stages of Consciousness: Meditations on the Boundaries of the Soul*, Great Barrington, MA: Lindisfarne Books, 1984.

Leivegoed, Bernard, *Man on the Threshold: The Challenge of Inner Development*, Stroud, UK: Hawthorn Press, 1985.

Lipson, Michael, *Stairway of Surprise: Six Steps to a Creative Life*, Great Barrington, MA: Anthroposophic Press, 2002.

Lowndes, Florin, *Enlivening the Chakra of the Heart: The Fundamental Spiritual Exercises of Rudolf Steiner*, London: Sophia Books, 1998.

Luxford, Michael, *Children with Special Needs: Rudolf Steiner's Ideas in Practice*, Great Barrington, MA: Anthroposophic Press, 1994.

Scaligero, Massimo, *The Light (La Luce): An Introduction to Creative Imagination*, Great Barrington, MA: Lindisfarne Books, 2001.

Smit, Jörgen, *Meditation: Bringing Change into Your Life*, London, Sophia Books, 1996.

Steiner, Rudolf, *Anthroposophy (A Fragment): A New Foundation for the Study of Human Nature*, Great Barrington, MA: Anthroposophic Press, 1996.

———, *Anthroposophy and the Inner Life: An Esoteric Introduction*, London: Rudolf Steiner Press, 1994.

———, *Anthroposophy in Everyday Life*, Great Barrington, MA: Anthroposophic Press, 1995.

———, *At Home in the Universe: Exploring Our Suprasensory Nature*, Great Barrington, MA: Anthroposophic Press, 2000.

———, *Broken Vessels: The Spiritual Structure of Human Frailty*, Great Barrington, MA: SteinerBooks, 2003.

———, *Christianity as Mystical Fact*, Great Barrington, MA: Anthroposophic Press, 1996.

———, *Cosmic Memory: Prehistory of Earth and Man*, Blauvelt, NY: Garber, 1987.

———, *Education for Special Needs: The Curative Education Course*, London: Rudolf Steiner Press, 1998.

———, *The Effects of Esoteric Development*, Great Barrington, MA: Anthroposophic Press, 1997.

———, *First Steps in Inner Development*, Great Barrington, MA, 1999.

———, *Freud, Jung, & Spiritual Psychology*, Great Barrington, MA: Anthroposophic Press, 2001 (previous edition, *Psychoanalysis and Spiritual Psychology*).

———, *The Healing Process: Spirit, Nature, and Our Bodies*, Great Barrington, MA: Anthroposophic Press, 2000.

————, *How to Know Higher Worlds: The Classic Guide to the Spiritual Journey,* Great Barrington, MA: Anthroposophic Press, 2002.

————, *Human and Cosmic Thought,* Great Barrington, MA: Anthroposophic Press, 1991.

————, *Introducing Anthroposophical Medicine,* Great Barrington, MA: Anthroposophic Press, 1999.

————, *Intuitive Thinking as a Spiritual Path: A Philosophy of Freedom,* Great Barrington, MA: Anthroposophic Press, 1995.

————, *Love and Its Meaning in the World,* Great Barrington, MA: Anthroposophic Press, 1998.

————, *Old and New Methods of Initiation,* London: Rudolf Steiner Press, 1991.

————, *An Outline of Esoteric Science,* Great Barrington, MA: Anthroposophic Press, 1998.

————, *A Psychology of Body, Soul, and Spirit: Anthroposophy, Psychosophy, Pneumatosophy,* Great Barrington, MA: Anthroposophic Press, 1999.

————, *Self-Transformation: Selected Lectures,* London: Rudolf Steiner Press, 1995.

————, *Sleep and Dreams: A Bridge to the Spirit,* Great Barrington, MA: Steiner Books, 2003.

————, *The Spiritual Guidance of the Individual and Humanity,* Great Barrington, MA: Anthroposophic Press, 1991.

————, *Theosophy: An Introduction to the Spiritual Processes in Human Life and in the Cosmos,* Great Barrington, MA: Anthroposophic Press, 1994.

————, *Three Streams in the Evolution of Mankind: The Connection of the Luciferic-Ahrimanic Impulses with the Christ-Jahve Impulse,* London: Rudolf Steiner Press, 1965.

————, *A Way of Self-Knowledge,* Great Barrington, MA: Anthroposophic Press, 1999.

————, *What is Anthroposophy?* Great Barrington, MA: Anthroposophic Press, 2002.

WILLIAM R. BENTO has worked within the fields of human development for more than thirty years. He is a recognized pioneer and published author in psychosophy (soul wisdom) and astrosophy (star wisdom) and travels extensively as a speaker, teacher, and consultant. He lives in Palo Alto, California.

CPSIA information can be obtained at www.ICGtesting.com
Printed in the USA
BVOW07s2130090315

390933BV00001B/4/P